Gypsy World

Gypsy World

The Silence of the Living and the

Voices of the Dead

PATRICK WILLIAMS

Translated by Catherine Tihanyi

THE UNIVERSITY OF CHICAGO PRESS
Chicago and London

PATRICK WILLIAMS is Director of Research at the CNRS (Centre
National de la Recherche Scientifique). His numerous publications
on Gypsy groups include *Mariage Tsigane* (1984); *Tsiganes: Identité,
évolution* (1989, as editor); *Les Tsiganes de Hongrie et leurs
musiques* (1996); and *Django* (1998).

CATHERINE TIHANYI, an anthropologist and translator, is a research
associate in the Department of Anthropology at Western Washing-
ton University.

THE UNIVERSITY OF CHICAGO PRESS, CHICAGO 60637
THE UNIVERSITY OF CHICAGO PRESS, LTD., LONDON
© 2003 by The University of Chicago
All rights reserved. Published 2003
Printed in the United States of America

12 11 10 09 08 07 06 05 04 03   1 2 3 4 5
ISBN: 0-226-89928-4 (cloth)
ISBN: 0-226-89929-2 (paperback)

Originally published as *Nous, on n'en parle pas: Les vivants et les
morts chez les Manouches* (Paris: Editions de la Maison des Sciences de l'Homme, 1993). © 1993, Ministère de l'Education na-
tionale et de la Culture, Mission du Patrimoine ethnologique.

Library of Congress Cataloging-in-Publication Data
Williams, Patrick, 1947–
    [Nous, on n'en parle pas. English]
    Gypsy world : the silence of the living and the voices of the
dead / Patrick Williams ; translated by Catherine Tihanyi.
        p.   cm.
    Includes bibliographical references and index.
    ISBN: 0-226-89928-4 (cloth : alk. paper)
    ISBN: 0-226-89929-2 (pbk. : alk. paper)
    1. Romanies—France—Social life and customs. 2. France—
Ethnic relations.   I. Title.
DX227.W5613 2003
393′.9′08991497044—dc21

                                              2002012707

To Nīni, in memoriam

CONTENTS

Mānuš Phonological Table

	Consonants					
Obstruents	voiceless	p	t	c	č	k
	aspirated	ph	th	—	—	kh
	voiced	b	d	—	ǯ (dž)	g
	glottal fricative	h				
Fricative	voiceless	f	s	š	x	
	voiced	v	z	(ž)	r	
Nasal		m	n			
Liquids		l	r			

	Vowels				
Short	a	e	i	o	u
Long	ā	ē	ī	ō	ū*

See Calvet, Delvoye, and Labalette 1970 for more details.

*The following are the approximate sound values in English for those consonants and vowels whose pronunciation is different than in English:

Consonants: [c] as in "ts" in "tsar"; [č] as in "ch" in "church"; [ǯ] or [dž] as in "j" in "Joe"; [š] as in "sh" in "shoot"; [x] as in "ch" in "Bach"; [ž] as in "s" in "pleasure."

Vowels: [a] as in "a" in "bat"; [e] as in "u" in "up"; [i] as in "e" in "be"; [o] as in "oa" in "oak"; [u] as in "oo" in "roost." Long vowels have different phonological values than short ones.

[j] and [w] are two allophones of [i] and [u], that is, they are pronounced in almost the same way as [i] and [u] and they appear at different places in words, but the meaning of Mānuš words is not dependent on these variations.

[ž] only appears in some titles in the bibliography. — *Trans.*

PHOTOGRAPHS

1. Photo by Michèle Brabo, 1969. Puy-de-Dôme.
2. Photo by Raymond Claquin, 1970 or 1971.
3. Photo by Raymond Claquin, 1970 or 1971.
4. Photo by Gérard Rondeau, n.d. On the shore of the Allier.
5. Photo by Raymond Claquin, 1975.
6. Photo by Raymond Claquin, 1975.
7. Photo by Michèle Brabo, 1969. Puy-de-Dôme.
8. Photo by Gérard Rondeau, n.d. Indre.
9. Photo by Gérard Rondeau, n.d.
10. Photo by Gérard Rondeau, n.d.
11. Photo by Gérard Rondeau, 1981.
12. Photo by Gérard Rondeau, n.d.
13. Photo by Michèle Brabo, 1969. Puy-de-Dôme. Pilgrimage on the steps of the church of Orcival. [According to Patrick Williams, men and women separate themselves in distinct groups on religious occasions.—*Trans.*]
14. Photo by Gérard Rondeau, 1982. Puy-de-Dôme.
15. Photo by Gérard Rondeau, 1982. Torpes.
16. Photo by Gérard Rondeau, 1982. Issoire.
17. Photo by Gérard Rondeau, 1982. Issoire.
18. Photo by Gérard Rondeau, 1982. Clermont-Ferrand.
19. Photo by Raymond Claquin, 1980. Saint-Dier d'Auvergne.
20. Photo by Raymond Claquin, 1975. Clermont-Ferrand.
21. Photo by Gérard Rondeau, 1982.
22. Photo by Gérard Rondeau, 1982.

TRANSLATOR'S ACKNOWLEDGMENTS

There are some very minor differences in this translated edition from the original French book, motivated by the need to clarify some official French practices for American readers.

I would like to express my heartfelt thanks to Patrick Williams for so generously answering my questions and reviewing the final draft of the translation. My thanks go also to T. David Brent for entrusting me with this translation and for his kind encouragements, to Russell D. Harper for his outstanding copyediting of this book and his contribution to the elucidation of some key concepts, and to Vladimir Milicic for his linguistic help in translating the phonological table.

ONE

Pre-text

We can often achieve a better perception of a reality we might have pondered for years when we come to peruse different horizons. Though I have known the Mānuš from the time of my childhood, I am not sure that, had it not been for the discussion Leonardo Piasere initiated with Judith Okely about the relations between the living and the dead among the Slovensko Roma (Piasere 1985) and the Traveller-Gypsies (Okely 1983), I would have thought of proposing that the terms of Mānuš presence in the world could be traced through the relationship of the living with the dead. It is not that these two authors' descriptions can be transposed to "my" field. All three of us have criticized applying to all Gypsies[1] observations made in one group and have instead insisted on the need to look at each group with new eyes. But Okely and Piasere evoke men and women who face the world with the same questions as the Mānuš do, and their analyses give the Gypsies of the southeast of England and the Slovensko Roma from the north of Italy portraits echoing each other. What particularly struck me when I systematically researched the relations between the living and the dead was not so much the coherence of the interpretations I could draw from them as my deeply felt loyalty to something I experienced when I was with the Mānuš. There is no halfway position for observers: we have to be either completely in or irremediably out, unable to grasp anything. The position of privileged observer is totally illusory. It is not even possible to touch upon the surface of things since, as I will try to show, Mānuš things do not have a surface. We either get to the bottom or nowhere at all: this is what the nature of the expression of Mānuš identity requires of the ethnologist, and it is a difficult ambition to live up to.

But once this difficulty is accepted, another one appears, one that too stems from that which is most fundamental in the situation of the

I

Mānuš—their presence in our midst. Science makes two sets of demands upon us: that of faithfully recording observations and that of bringing to light the organization and functioning of the observed phenomena. In this case, faithfulness requires showing that the essence of the observed phenomena cannot be grasped. How could I write in such a way as to convey an understanding even while respecting this ungraspable primordial nature? I propose the following answer: to show everything, to tell everything. I propose seeking and, I might even dare say, achieving absolute pertinence, complete coincidence. Nothing should be left out, nothing should be added: there should be no breach through which a disregard of Mānuš plenitude could penetrate. The Mānuš ideal is to take possession of the universe without disturbing anything in it.

But the very ambition of achieving this brings trouble. Gestures, words, and the attitudes I report constitute a Mānuš discourse, a discourse on the world. My exposition is unavoidably a commentary. If I wish to reconstitute Mānuš totality as I uncover it, as a compact bloc that cannot be fractured, I will have to place it in its context and proceed in two stages. The first will pertain to the dead among the living (from a point of view internal to the Mānuš community), the second, to the Mānuš among the Gadzos[2] (here we observe the Mānuš within the broader society).

And yet I cannot prevent the second part from appearing as a deployment, an explanation of the first. Already, the Mānuš construction has been breached and silence has been shattered.

THE FAMILIES I WILL TALK ABOUT and that I have encountered in the Central Massif have been marked by a centuries-long stay in German-speaking territories. Genealogical studies (Valet 1986; Reyniers 1992) show that the Mānuš from the Auvergne and Limousin regions have ancestors who for the most part lived in Alsace, Hesse, and Westphalia.[3] Their arrival in France was gradual and scattered; it occurred during the second half of the nineteenth century and continued through the beginning of the twentieth. The reasons for the migration of these families who all still have members in Alsace are not clear, though the 1870 war between France and Prussia probably speeded up this exodus even though it did not trigger it. Today, we encounter Mānuš of Germanic origin throughout France. Prior to the movement of urbanization that led them to congregate near towns at the end of the nineteen sixties, they seemed to prefer to stay in certain rural areas such as woodlands and foothills: Alsace, Béarn, Basse-Normandie, Central Massif . . . They arrived in Auvergne and Limousin by following various itineraries: some came through Belgium, others through Switzerland, and others yet through the Loire and Berry regions . . . However, it does seem that, once they reached their present location, they stayed put. Most of them have been wandering for two, three, sometimes even four or more generations in these two or three *départements,* in some cases in only two or three cantons. When the oldest ones are asked why they chose these areas, they answer as follows: because there was brush, because there were hedgehogs, because there was pasture for the horses, because there were rivers with trout, because the peasants were giving them hay, bacon and milk, because there were springs on the mountainsides and fountains in the villages . . . The younger ones answer that they stay here because their elders lived and are buried here.

These Mānuš thus have cousins in the whole of France, and yet at present they make up a specific entity in relation to the other Mānuš of France. They prefer to marry among themselves and have some cultural traits that differentiate them, as for instance some aspects of their dialect. Mānuš language is still their everyday language, the first one their children learn to speak—which is no longer the case in many other communities.

This rural zone is bordered by a number of average-sized towns that Mānuš usually avoid visiting, except for hospital or prison stays, or to take care of administrative formalities. Limoges lies to the west, Montluçon to the north, Vichy and Thiers are to the east, while to the south the towns of Le Puy, Aurillac, and Brive form a straight line. This area covers approximately the *départements* of Puy-de-Dôme, Creuse, Corrèze, Haute-Vienne, and part of Haute-Loire, Allier, and Cantal. But, even though family networks do indeed cover all of this area and though the families that we will meet all live in it, there are few among them whose circuits take them from one farthest boundary to another, except for unusual events such as funerals. In the nineteen eighties, the Mānuš population might have been three thousand. I will be concerned more specifically with the families whose usual circuit is limited to Limagne d'Allier and Combrailles.

TWO

Mare Mūle: The Dead among the Living

Why speak of the "presence" of the dead among the living when, as soon as the deceased is buried, in accordance with present-day French norms, Mānuš gestures all seem aimed at confirming the physical disappearance by insuring the disappearance of all traces and memories that might remind the living of the deceased? The Mānuš' most spectacular gestures, the ones they talk about, the ones they present as their traditions, are aimed at giving absence its full weight, at establishing its definitive nature in all domains. This is our way, they say, this is how it must be done.

THE WEALTH AND BELONGINGS OF THE DECEASED

Nothing should be kept, say the Mānuš. Indeed, the deceased's trailer is set in flames along with its contents, including at times the departed's car or truck. Any jewelry or money that has not been given away before his or her death is buried along with the remains or is used to pay for the funeral or to decorate the grave. Occasionally, less spectacular practices than fire are resorted to. The trailer and vehicle might be sold, but only to a Gadzo and without trying to make a good deal (the money thus acquired will be spent "on the graves"), or they might be given or sold to a junkyard, and the family makes sure they are destroyed and not recycled. Whether they be burnt, destroyed or sold, no ritual gesture, no special words, accompany the disappearance of these valued objects. But it can also happen that the belongings of the dead are kept, though this can only apply to part of them, never to the whole. Any sort of object could be kept. At times there are obvious practical reasons for this: a poor widow with lots of children will keep the trailer, the car, or the truck (those who can afford it prefer to destroy them, but, in spite of their need, Rikela, Bātour's widow, and their children chose to burn the father's trailer and end up "on foot"). As money is held in common by a couple, the widow or widower can keep the part not used to pay for the funeral (but it is rare that this money is used later on for any other purpose than to decorate graves). But an object that is kept could also be a knife, a guitar, a watch, tools (wrench, screwdriver, sharpening stone . . .), a rifle; it could be anything the defunct used often and that she or he was attached to, including a favorite dog, a crow or other birds, and, in the olden days, a horse. These objects that are preserved can be used, as any ordinary thing in everyday life; but then again, the trailer can be parked with no one living in it, no longer traveling. One can wear the ring of one's "defunct father," or it can be carefully tied into a shawl and stored in a drawer and never shown in public again. Whether they remain in use or out of circulation, all the objects that belonged to a deceased and are kept are *mulle* (*mūle-le, -mūle-ile-, mūlo-lo, -mūlo-ilo, i mulles:* dead objects, a deceased's objects, the dead, it's dead). Anything *mullo* must be treated "with respect," *unti vel ēra,* "there must be respect" — a phrase that comes up all the time. "There must be respect," that is, it must not be neglected, mistreated, abandoned, and particularly not lost. In a widow's trailer, one must not curse, use crude words, argue. A *mullo* dog should not be insulted or beaten. A *mullo* horse has to be kept till its natural death. And moreover, when the family stops using these objects, they will not meet the fate of ordinary objects that can be exchanged, sold, or thrown away, but rather that of objects that had belonged to a departed. They will be destroyed.

Thus, when three years after his death, Runda's widow and children decided to get rid of his truck (it was at the end of its rope but had been kept for obvious reasons of social and economic survival: they needed it to pull the trailer they used for their work of collecting metal scraps), they gave it to a junkyard: "We had it put in the compactor, that's the way to do it," the family states. Not being able to insure that the object would be respected, that is to say, that the truck would be maintained in good condition, they chose to destroy it.

And yet, except for their final destinations, there is nothing that differentiate *mulle* objects from ordinary ones in the course of everyday life. They are mixed with others without any distinguishing mark. There is no clue to differentiate a *mullo* dog sleeping among all the other dogs under the trailer. In the same way, how could we know that those fiberglass

chimney-sweeping sticks so sought after by the practitioners of the trade
and which have been set down across the V-shaped hitch of a parked
trailer are *mulle?* The widow lays them out this way at each stop and only
those who knew her husband well can guess their nature. This is because
there is no specific way of handling *mulle* objects, as they are not usually
referred to as such. Mānuš do not announce that such and such a thing
is *mulli.* This is not silence in response to an outsider's curiosity, that of
an ethnographer, for example, but it is indeed a silence at play among
members of the group. Pīpini refused to lend his *pétanque*[1] balls to his
cousin, who had asked to borrow them for a competition; in fact these
were *mulle* balls, they had belonged to his "defunct father," and Pīpini
was afraid that, if his cousin didn't play as well as he hoped for, he might
swear at or insult the balls. But Pīpini said nothing and refused without
any explanation: his lack of generosity and solidarity (two valued quali-
ties) were met with disapproval.

The silence around *mulle* objects is only a specific aspect of the general silence surrounding the dead. *Me, rakā gar ap u kuč mūle,* "Our
poor dead! We don't talk about them," "One must not speak of the
dead." So in what way does one not talk about them?

The Names of the Defunct and Their Evocation

In order to describe the attitude of the living toward the memory of a
dead person (the evocation of her or his appearance, of the events and
actions that have marked her or his life), I need to distinguish between
time and kinship, and this in terms of nearness and distance from the
death.

The first distinction simply pertains to temporal distance. The period
close to the event of death (*bari trāva,* "deep mourning") is differentiated
from the period distant from it—I will come back to the vagueness of
these terms. This is not a sharp differentiation, as we are in a continuum.
Secondly, there is differentiation between closeness or distance among
the living, that is, between the deceased's close kin and others—and here
too the term "differentiation" is not really appropriate, as these limits
are not set in an absolute manner.

Who are the close kin of the deceased? They are firstly the blood relatives, classified the same way as in the overall French population. These
include children, brothers and sisters, spouse, cousins. In addition, any

member of the group able to uncover some sort of kinship tie and having been close to the departed could decide to consider herself or himself a close kin. Attitudes pertaining to the evocation of the deceased vary from one period to the next, then, according to whether individuals consider themselves close to or distant from the dead.

For months (though it could be for years, the "closer" someone is to the deceased the longer it takes) following the death, the "close" kin stop uttering the name of the deceased and stop evoking his or her memory: "We don't talk about our dead." The norm is stated as universal and always pertains to the "close" kin and the period of "deep mourning." In contrast, this is a time when there is much talk about the dead beyond the circle of "close" kin. As they are spreading news of the death, people reminisce about the events the deceased experienced, and her or his name is pronounced frequently, though always accompanied by a formula said to be one of "respect," *u kuč Kālo,* "the defunct Kālo."

Then gradually over a number of years the departed is evoked less often in the community; his or her name is uttered more rarely, while the members of the defunct's close circle gradually allow themselves to reminisce. But they always do so with much vigilance and precaution. Among these precautions is the one prohibiting referring to the deceased by name, unless the name be framed by proper respectful formulas (not "Kālo" but "my poor defunct Kālo"). There are many who prefer not to utter the defunct's name at all (thus "my poor defunct brother," "my defunct father," and for a widow, *mur kuč čorelo,* "my poor unfortunate one," "my poor defunct husband," or simply "my poor defunct"). Sometimes the departed's name was that of an object, a quality, or an animal. In that case circumlocutions are resorted to (*Kālo* becomes *k ilo gar vejs,* "that which is not white," *Hāzo,* "hare," becomes *U lolo ke našela sik,* "the red one who runs fast" . . .).

The dead are not called by their names, which means that the living and the dead are not present in the same way among the living. Because in normal everyday conversation, the names of individuals being addressed are constantly uttered. This privileging, this affection for given names, is one of the more striking aspects of Mānuš speech ("Nīni, you've forgotten to turn off the car lights, Nīni," "*Oh Je Garçounet! Garçounet ap dox te xas mancax mur Garçounet,* "Oh You Garçounet, Garçounet come eat with me, my Garçounet"). To address a dead person in

the same manner as one would a living one would be equivalent to using a *mullo* object carelessly. All these prescriptions are presented and
explained in terms of "respect," *ēra*. This care can be seen for instance
when a person who started to reminisce suddenly stops and becomes
silent or when he or she is reticent to begin such an evocation. The reason
that is then given is that the speaker is afraid of making a mistake (*te
xoxap,* "of lying," "of making a mistake"), of not be able to remember
the events and their participants exactly as they were, of being unfaith-
ful to them. *Te xoxap gar ap leste,* "let me not lie in any way about him,"
is a propitiatory invocation frequently used before telling a story about
the deceased. When telling about things that involve the departed, past
reality and its depiction in the present must coincide perfectly.

And indeed, when a kin starts to recount memories, we can assume
that this coincidence does exist, that it seems sufficient to give the speaker
the feeling that it does exist, that the speaker is faithful to the past and
doesn't expose herself or himself to the risk of being contradicted or
corrected. That the speaker respects her or his dead. So, when a seventy-
nine-year-old woman (born November 1911), widowed for forty years,
begins to narrate episodes from the time of her "poor defunct" (whose
name she never utters)—and she does so with the certainty that she is
telling events the way they were—we have to assume that, while for years
she never evoked him in public, she must have often evoked him in her
mind when she was alone. And when Tatoun, while drinking with his
camp buddies a little more than two years after his father's death, starts
to sing the deceased's favorite song, one that no one in the family has
sung since the death, and has no trouble remembering the exact lyrics
of three long couplets in French (it is a "realist" song of the nineteen
twenties, filled with action), but this without raising his voice, so that his
mother sleeping in a nearby trailer won't hear him, we again have to sup-
pose that, during these past two years, his "poor father's" song too must
have often played in his head.

A public and a private sphere emerge when we follow the trajectory
of the memory and the name of a deceased. Two entities come into view:
the group and the individual. The evocation of the dead passes from one
to the other.

We can see this dialectic between group and individual permeate
every aspect of mourning. Indeed, there is always a combination of a

normative aspect (there are things that must be done when one is in mourning: women must dress in black for instance, while there are things that should not be done, such as listening to music, watching TV . . .) with an aspect left to individual initiative (even though it is said that one should publicly mourn close kin for a year, and even two if one wants to show how attached one was to her or him, each person can, without needing to publicly state any reason, shorten or lengthen their mourning period, and this without any specific ceremony—simply, she might throw away her black clothes, or he might turn on the TV again in the trailer, and let others think what they may). Thus the mourning periods that I have outlined, vague as they are, should also be considered variable: mourning lasts for the time mourners decide, and they each make their own decision.

We have seen that this was also the case for the boundaries of the group of mourners, as each kin decides whether or not to consider herself or himself "close." Only spouses, children, and siblings have no choice in the matter. So even though the norm does have meaning, it never succeeds in establishing a rigorous and universal code. Black is the color of deep mourning for women. As time goes by and the time of the death recedes, women take their distance from black, passing through gray, then purple, navy blue, then maroon, blue, beige, lighter and lighter up to white, then greens, reds, multicolored materials, and golden ornaments that some women never wear again. But I only noticed this in the course of much observation and many meetings. For instance, a woman whom I last encountered dressed in black might now be dressed in gray and purple, and the same for another woman, and another . . . Looking at a group conversing in front of a trailer, it becomes apparent that women who recently lost a father or a brother or a husband are not wearing the same colors as the others . . . But there is no formal prescription for this, there never is unanimity in the practice, and of course it would be erroneous to say that specific colors are automatically linked to set times following deaths.

THE PART LEFT TO INDIVIDUAL INITIATIVE can be clearly seen in another series of gestures through which the living show their respect for the dead. These pertain to what we might call "the things of this world the defunct was fond of."

Close kin, during the mourning period and sometimes for the rest of their lives, will stop consuming something the dead was fond of. This is manifested mostly through prohibitions that we could as well call homage. Prohibitions can apply to food or drink—the bereaved ceases eating or drinking something the departed was fond of—but the bereaved can also stop singing the song the dead person used to sing during celebrations, stop telling his or her favorite stories, cease listening to the music he or she liked, no longer frequent the spots the dead used to enjoy (such as a café, a village, the shore of a river . . .), or renounce what used to be the defunct's preferred activity (trout fishing, playing belotte . . .). It seems clear that individuals can choose their own prohibitions. Very often mourners will give up something that used to be appreciated by both the defunct and themselves, and at times mourners will abstain from something they are personally fond of, as they feel that this is the best way to show respect. And even though the range of foods and drinks and activities of these Mānuš is not very broad (most often the prohibition will be drinking wine or eating wild boar—though some will specify a specific recipe for grilled or braised wild boar . . .), the tastes of the deceased and the choices of the living are still varied enough to make any kind of item the object of prohibition or homage.

There is yet another aspect to these gestures; it involves sharing with the dead. The mourner at times makes a gesture that is the inversion of abstinence, he or she, when drinking wine, beer, brandy, etc., pours a few drops on the ground before drinking, saying "it's for my departed." This same gesture is performed when taking an oath and calling upon one's dead as witness: *mur mūle te* . . . , "on my dead if . . ." The renouncing of a given food, drink, or activity isn't accompanied by any sort of public declaration. Nothing is said. Individuals choose and respect the prohibitions they pick for themselves, and they don't have to tell anyone about them. I have never heard anyone refuse a dish or a drink with the explanation that they were doing this out of respect for a deceased. At any rate, there is hardly any difference between *xō gar* and *xō pu gar* ("I don't eat this" and "I don't eat this anymore"). Just as they can decide the appropriate time to utter the names of the dead or evoke them, individuals can, when they feel it is appropriate, end the prohibitions they imposed on themselves. Again there is no need to make a formal declaration to others, to those who might have noticed that the period of abstinence has ended.

While all of these gestures confirm an individual's death, they are also specific ways of installing him or her among the living. These ways lead to the creation of an amnesiac community, albeit one made up of individuals who do have memories. It seems clear that the manner in which the process of commemoration is organized leads to the preservation of memories that are more and more intimate and in no way encourages the construction of a common memory, a saga memory, an epic memory, a memory of the group as group. The only support for group memory and group self-knowledge lies in interactions among individuals. Their homage eliminates monuments more than it builds them. It is characterized by being made up of ordinary objects kept in ordinary use, generating no particular discourse, or else taken out of the public sphere and then only functioning as a support to a discourse in the private sphere.

But what of the traces left by the Mānuš in the technologies of memory preservation in Gadzo society,[2] such as registers, books, newspapers, trial transcripts, and ordinances? These only store the memory of what the Mānuš have let the Gadzo know or see. In the eyes of the Mānuš, they don't matter. The Mānuš never call upon them when interacting with each other. However, there are two recent exceptions to this: photographs and audio tapes. The pictures of the dead decorate trailer walls (though they only appear gradually after the death), and the occupants are required to insure these images are respected. Thus great care is taken when circulating these pictures.[3] In the recent past, audio tapes used to be destroyed, but they are now preserved (though this does not mean they are played very often).[4]

These attitudes tempt me to conclude that the Mānuš choose oblivion over memory. But oblivion isn't empty. The dead do disappear—and in the end they disappear rapidly. Given these practices it is not surprising that genealogical memory is reduced to four generations, which, taking into account early marriages and childbearing, represent only a short span of time. Added to this, the Mānuš die young. But, though they disappear as Bimba, Nōno, Majblum, or Fayola, they do remain as kin within the community. Though the "forgotten" dead who used to be known has become anonymous, he or she has not departed from the community of the living. The living aim to keep the dead in the community though their gestures. The Mānuš group is made up of the living as much as of the dead. There is a Mānuš memory but it is a memory that shuns speechmaking, a memory that isn't aimed at exploring the past and accumulating knowledge. "Respect," *ēra,* is, for the Mānuš, the form taken by what we call memory.

It is out of respect that the dead are not evoked or only evoked with extreme precaution. "So as to avoid making a mistake about him," *te na xoxap ap leste,* Tchāvo always announces when beginning a story about "the time of my poor father." The possibility of mistake torments the living. He explains that the need to make corrections would torment the dead, error would be a breach of "respect," which in this situation involves the dead's tranquility, the breaching of which would drive the deceased in turn to trouble the tranquility of the living. The reason a departed's possessions have to be destroyed or used as *mulle* objects, that is, with "respect," lies in the need for integrity: one should not step in someone else's tracks, or, when evoking the past, one should take extreme care to not change these traces in any way. This destruction of the possessions of the dead, the using up of all of the money the departed left behind on the grave, the absence of any public explanation for all the gestures pertaining to the dead (not being explicit is the best sign of faithfulness)—these are all ways of establishing a silence that is not empty. Each individual is uniquely irreplaceable. (Judith Okely mentions the horror of transplants among British Gypsies, which leads them to refuse to leave the bodies of their loved ones in the hospital or the morgue. I find the same feeling among the Mānuš—the same fear of doctors secretly amputating the body to take an organ—and the same resolve to take their deceased brother or sister from the hospital so as to watch the body themselves during the wake.) And yet, this individual uniqueness is associated with the absolute coincidence of generations: we are Mānuš, we are what Mānuš have always been.

Put in these terms, the relation between the living and the dead doesn't involve a chronological temporal dimension. The "respect" for the dead opens not onto the past but onto the immutable. There is no room for the accidents of history. It is thus wrong to say that the departed leaves nothing for the living. The dead leave behind, in addition to community solidarity requiring the absence of family inheritance, the insurance of the incorruptibility of their Mānuš identity. The dead turn the living into members of the group. Though the living strive to maintain loyalty, they do not evoke its object, or they do so in specific ways that make of it a private evocation, one that becomes gradually more intimate, fated to disappear along with those who knew the defunct. The same process that leads individuals to anonymity also manifests that which is irreplaceable in them. The deceased ends up losing his or her unique characteristics, but there remains a loyalty to an entity, the group, the Mānuš, "us," of which the dead now collectively and anonymously insure the survival. We are that which our dead made us and, since our homage consists in loyalty to the defunct rather than in preserving a memory apt to be constituted into history, we are what our dead made of us for all times and without fail. Loyalty endures even while memory cannot be preserved.

In this way the dead construct the community without its having to go through the construction of a history of the community. I would like to argue that what the Mānuš call "the respect for the dead" is actually integrity, the integrity of the social group at all its levels.

A lexical study could support this argument. Among the Mānuš there is a word for "respect," *ēra*, but there is no word for "memory." In order to say "I remember," the verb "to think" (*tengrōva*) is used and this in its impersonal form (*tengrel man, tengrel tut?* "it remembers to me, does it remember to you?"[5] so that when they speak French we hear *ça me souvient, t'en souvient-il? . . .* ["this reminds me, does it remind you?" . . .]),[6] as if memory were not a purposeful activity controlled by the subject but something that occurs involuntarily, like the return of the dead. Joseph Valet ([1971] 1986) gives to *ēra* the meaning of respect toward the dead and of honor toward the living.[7]

But I will choose another example to back the proposition that "respect" is equivalent to the integrity of the group. It pertains to exchanges of insults invoking the dead. These insults always evoke eating (*xa tur mūlen!* "eat your dead!") or copulation (*Dō buje tur mūlen!* "I fuck your dead!"). The insult that thus brings the dead into play is an act that is different from any other sort of insult or aggression. If two individuals quarrel and insult each other, they might come to blows and stop seeing each other, or they might forget everything a few days later: the incident will have no lasting consequences for the community. But if, during the argument, individual *a* insults the dead of *b,* it is then all the *B*s, all those who are attached to the same dead as *b,* who will be up in arms. (It must be remembered that the boundaries of this group are fuzzy, since to be attached to a particular dead is an individual decision, and it is thus not possible, for instance, to equate this group to a set of agnates, as cognatic ties are also taken into account: I may decide to respect and to demand respect for dead from my mother's side as much as those from my father's. This means that such a group only comes into effective existence when its dead are insulted.)

It might happen that *a*'s kin feel that *a* committed an irreparable act too lightly. In that case they will disassociate themselves from the guilty party by publicly expressing their disapproval of his or her action. This might satisfy the *B*s. When the aptly named Tarzan took the place of his weak and sickly brother Mōzo to retaliate against the young husband of one of Mōzo's sisters who publicly insulted Mōzo "and all his race,"[8] no one objected. But should the *B*s in turn insult *a*'s dead, then the *A*s will mobilize and there will be war. In cases of conflict, an insult to the dead, or more often the threat alone of an insult to the dead, is a sign that the individual involved is not afraid of the conflict spreading to the whole of the group and starting a war (it is not rare for these exchanges of insults to end in exchange of rifle fire).

On the other hand, brothers or cousins can play at mutually insulting their dead without any consequences—it's like playing with fire, but it's still a game. But this sort of game stops, as the Mānuš put it, as soon as there are *freš mūle,* "fresh dead," that is, recent dead. Gugui and Doudou were the sons of two brothers, and they generously and reciprocally insulted their dead while their fathers were alive. It was a way of flaunting their fraternity, to reiterate that they had the same dead. But after one of the fathers died, they stopped. Such insult would provoke war. The subsequent death of the other father didn't reestablish the initial situation.

Thus, in peace as in war, no entity can be constituted outside of the presence of the dead. Just as it's only from the moment an object becomes *mullo* that it truly belongs to an individual ("the defunct Tata's guitar," *i puška fun u kuč Djangela*—"poor Djangela's rifle"), a Mānuš gathers a group around her or him at the moment of death. The boundary between the inside and outside of the group is laid out through the game of insults: We—the Others. And in every case, it is the breach inflicted to the integrity of the group (represented by the "respect" for the dead) that provokes war.

These attitudes are reminiscent of others I evoked earlier—for instance, not buying a trailer in which someone has died and not selling such a vehicle to other Mānuš: these too are part of the same play as insults, here too the integrity of the group is at issue. This also brings to mind the ludic character of repartees within the community: everyone is ready to say of the others that they are "great liars" or, with a touch of admiration, that "this guy's an even a bigger liar than me!" It's a game. But when someone involves the dead in his or her words—by swearing on one's dead, on one's "poor father"—the truth is ensured, the words are full, they have integrity, they are Mānuš. The group is indeed the living and the dead united, and the graves themselves proclaim this.

THE GRAVES "U GRĀBLI"

All the ethnographers and other observers of the Mānuš have been struck by the frequency of their visits to the tombs and the care with which they are maintained. These observers usually link these practices to the belief in *mūlo,* the "dead who come back," "the *revenants,*"[9] and the attendant fear of them. The care is explained by the need to keep the dead in their place. These latter, knowing that they have visitors, will not feel the need to go outside the boundaries assigned to them. I am not going along with this interpretation, as I would rather suggest that the tomb stands for the family group, the Mānuš group, and this as much as the departed's dwelling does. I am proposing, then, that the visibility of the group (of the tomb that stands for it) in Gadzo territory brings about the necessity for the extreme care devoted to grave sites.

The tombs are often imposing and expensive monuments, and this is remarkable given the precarious standard of living of these Mānuš families. The architecture of these tombs is no different from that of Gadzo tombs, but even those Mānuš tombs of relatively modest size stand out on account of the abundance of bouquets and trinkets. The Mānuš do not build individual tombs; they choose instead to have "family vaults" with four, six, or eight places in them. The tombstone usually only bears the inscription "family" followed by the family name. It is only recently that some families have engraved underneath this the official names ("the name for the Gadzo") and dates of the individuals buried there, sometimes adding their photographs. At all times graves are decorated with fresh or artificial flowers and a whole panoply of trinkets which are sold in specialty shops. These trinkets can be divided into four categories:

1. Reminders of kinship links. When there are several coffins in a tomb, nearly all close kinship links are mentioned on the trinkets: "to our father," "brother," "godfather," "uncle," "cousin," etc.

2. Objects expressing an individual loss: "ever since you left me, my eyes haven't stopped crying," "alone missing you."

3. Reminders that the living keep on thinking about the dead even when away from their graves. These include souvenirs of various visits to religious sites: "we prayed for you in the Sacred Grotto," "the *Curé* of Ars," etc.

4. Finally, objects that do not belong to the ordinary funerary decorum and stand for specific values. These are often the motifs of a horseshoe or a bronze horse (Okely and Piasere, who found that the groups they studied favored the same motifs, see them as symbol of traveling, of the Journey).

Mānuš tombs are often located in Gadzo cemeteries. They tend to be in the same part of the cemetery (kin like to be assembled in death: whenever possible, Mānuš favor sepulchral vaults that can contain six or eight people, and when they are filled up, the families look to the nearest available plot; when someone dies far away from the familial cemetery, long distances are traveled to bring the kin back . . .). Yet these tombs do not form enclaves: they are scattered among Gadzo graves, just as Mānuš trailers are scattered in Gadzo territory. But, while the trailers can be hidden from Gadzo gaze "behind bushes," "out of the way in the countryside," the houses of the dead remain permanently exposed.

It would be wrong to think that the Mānuš are not sensitive to Gadzo curiosity. All the flowers, the messages of love, the public display of family ties are aimed at presenting a group image to the Gadzo (the group as it exists only in the union-of-the-living-and-the-dead). The same happens during the only occasion when the Mānuš assemble in the street and show themselves to Gadzo gaze. The crowd at a funeral reveals the true dimension of the group and the solidarity of its members. The presence of all at funerals is again a matter of integrity: a missing relative would mean a breach within the group. When going to the cemetery, the Mānuš do not say they are on their way to visit a specific deceased but rather always use the expression *ǯā ap u grābli,* "We are going to visit the tombs." These visits to the grave sites are similar to the visits to the trailers. When stopping at a camp, relatives must be visited before anyone else, but afterwards everyone in the group must be greeted. In the cemetery, visitors first stop at their kin's graves and pay them their respect, but then they also pay respect to all the other Mānuš tombs in the cemetery. When traveling for leisure or work and passing through a locale where kin are buried, Mānuš are expected to stop and greet them, just as they do when unexpectedly meeting other Mānuš trailers on the road. The numbers of daily encounters experienced by the people staying in a campsite as well as by those traveling by car bears witness to the intensity of social life within the community. These meetings include those with dead as well as living kin. Both types of encounters are important in the constructing of Mānuš identity. The prescription to greet dead and living kin is so strong and the adhesion to it so total that Moršela, rather than traveling through a village or a town without stopping at the cemetery, preferred to make a detour to avoid it, this despite the urgency driving us to travel from one end of the *département* to the other.

People converse with the dead as they do with the living, and there are occasions when drinks are consumed over the tombs on certain religious celebrations, the first of January, for instance, or the deceased's birthdays . . . This doesn't mean that the dead are treated in a manner equivalent to the living. Visits to the dead do take into account their belonging to another plane. Individuals will visit even relatively distant tombs after a defunct appeared to them in a dream, or when troubles are suddenly "miraculously" resolved, or again when a wish has been fulfilled. All this comes easier for those living close to the tombs. This explains why the family sepulchral vault becomes the reference point in the territory. It is the dead that link the Mānuš to a given region.

The tombs are images of the group as much as they are "houses" of the dead, and this links up with another series of precautions that is required in regard to the deceased. These I will evoke next so as to complete the description of the relation with the dead in terms of space and particularly the mediating role played by the dead.

MŪLENGRE PLACI: "THE PLACES OF THE DEAD"

In contrast to the oft-visited tombs, the place where a kin dies ceases to be frequented. The explanation given is again of course that of "respect." Some of the bereaved also claim that they couldn't bear the images of

the defunct which the place would unavoidably conjure up. Like many of
the prescriptions pertaining to "respect," this one too calls for taking into
account proximity. In terms of temporal proximity, the place is avoided
during the months following the death. As time goes by, trailers will
again stop there, but the closer people were to the deceased the longer
they will avoid it. In terms of spatial proximity, the town or village where
the death occurred is avoided and so is the encampment. At the campsite, trailers will be moved a few meters away from the specific spot
where the death occurred. There is no particular term to designate these
places aside from *Ap i placa kaj našrum mur kuč čāvo,* "It's here that I
lost my poor deceased son," *Kote koj mujaslo u kuč Kālo,* "Here, where
my poor Kālo died." Likewise, no sign marks them. Those who knew the
deceased along with people passing through the area at the time of
death know their emplacement, while the others can find out from those
in the know. It seems that it is the event of the death that turns these
"places" into "places of death" that should be avoided.

There are also some places that are explicitly designated as *mūlengri
placa,* "the place of the dead." The Mānuš store *mulle* objects there.
Among those, the most noticeable items are the deceased's trailer, car,
or truck, when they have not been destroyed right after the death or
when they are no longer of use to the family. It seems that in this case the
places have been contaminated by the objects that then turn them into
mūlengre placi, "the places of the dead." Often the Mānuš own these
parcels, though their claim might lie more in the accumulation of *mulle*
objects on them than official deeds of ownership. This could be a parcel
that has been completely fenced off or it could be part of a lot where the
family spends a few months out of each year. This place doesn't become
forbidden—people do enter it now and then—but it does cease to be part
of the framework of everyday life. There are no specific ways of dealing
with this sort of parcel. The objects placed there are never put back in
circulation. The fate of a *mūlengri placa* lies midway between that of
mulle objects kept in use within the circuits of everyday life and which
call for a careful use, and that of the same sort of objects stored at the
back of a drawer and kept away from all gazes. Once again the best way
to show respect is to avoid touching these things. A *mūlengri placa* most
often resembles a place that has been abandoned. Gadzos are quite
shocked to see Mānuš families not living on a property they own (while

they are staying elsewhere in the commune in a space that is probably less comfortable and from all viewpoints less respectable as they don't own it), letting it get overgrown with weeds and allowing a trailer and car that used to be functional rot away on it. This neglect might appear permanent: the *mūlengri placa* remains the same (weeds keep on growing, vehicles keep on rusting), and the Gadzo wonders if the Mānuš family that owns it is still concerned with it. It can also happen that, after some time has elapsed, the objects stored there undergo the same fate as all *mulle* objects do: they are destroyed and the parcel is sold. It is very rare that a *mūlengri placa* partakes again of the movement of life. However, during the summer of 1986, Gantz (who had just converted to Pentecostalism) [10] put back into use the parcel that had belonged to old Lōri, his great-grandfather, and which hadn't been occupied since his death more than twenty years earlier. There was a certain amount of reticence among some family members, even among those who had also converted, and for once it was not "respect" for the dead that was invoked but fear of the *mūlo*.

The question of the *mūlo*, "the dead who comes back," needs to be settled. Authors dealing with death among the Mānuš and other "Gypsy" groups have been primarily and almost exclusively interested in the *mūlo* (Erdös 1959; Dollé 1970). Many useless questions have been asked: Is the *mūlo* a beneficent or a malevolent being? Why? Is it visible or invisible? Does it take the shape of the deceased or another form? Is it Gadzo or Mānuš? It seems possible to state (1) that the belief in the *mūlo* should not be seen as discrete from other things. This firstly because this very same word is used both for the defunct at peace, not tormented by anything, and for the dead who comes back. At any rate it is obvious that the dead can come back since they never cease to be present among the living! And (2), that the dead who comes back is thus perceived as an extraordinary or frightening instance of the presence of the dead among the living, as he or she comes back in a manner that the living cannot control. The *mūlo*'s appearance can take many forms: invisible, human, animal, or monstrous . . . The essence of this apparition is that it is uncontrollable.

These sorts of apparitions occur for two reasons. Firstly, the dead can come back in case of a death that was not peaceful, as all violent or accidental deaths can trigger unexpected *mūlo* apparitions. These dead coming back could be Gadzo as well as Mānuš. They crop up in stories of night travel; for example, in one about highway 941 between Pontau-mur and Pontgibaud, where a mūlo was seen in the form of a red-eyed dog barking and pursuing cars at eighty miles per hour. This sort of in-formation can lead people to change their itineraries. The second rea-son for the apparition of a *mūlo* is that the living did not show respect toward it. This lack of respect might have been accidental: there are sto-ries of trailers that have turned around during the night (in the morning the back end is where the front used to be) because the family, travel-ing in an area it was not familiar with, inadvertently camped on a spot where someone had died.[11] Lack of respect can also be intentional, for instance when someone might curse or invoke the dead needlessly (it isn't right "to constantly have the dead on the lips") or not properly care for *mulle* objects. The dead then react in ways similar to the living when their integrity is threatened: they suddenly mix with the living just as the living suddenly disturbed them. There are thus two kinds of *mūle,* the protectors and the frightening ones, the "good" and the "bad," just as there are two kinds of attitudes the living can have toward *mūle:* respect or lack of respect.

In other words, *mūle* are feared only when they are not respected. Matcho's family, in trouble with the local police, only visited its dead at night, thus showing their fear of the *gendarme* to be stronger than their fear of the mūlo. And yet, there is the constant and diffuse possibility of inadvertently disturbing an unknown dead. From this standpoint, and only from it, *mūle* are akin to the Gadzos. They are part of a universe the Mānuš strive to manage but which they can never be sure of having com-plete control over: danger—uncontrollable—can always spring up when least expected. A frequent motif in Mānuš tales is that of women who are traveling to sell their lace works or baskets: they knock at the door of an isolated building and "when the door opens . . ."

THE ADVENT OF THE MĀNUŠ

We now need to think about the whole of the observations I made in re-gard to the attitudes organizing the coexistence of the living and the dead. In all the domains where homage is rendered to the dead (that is, everywhere, as division into domains is only a rhetorical device), the same process is at play: it starts out with undifferentiated space, and then, from within this monotony, some marked elements are elected/selected, elements possessing a value calling for their acknowledgment. Most often there is nothing in particular that differentiates these elements from among all those encountered in that space. At times the Mānuš have constituted the homogeneity of that space; at others, it is simply their acceptance of that which exists, that which the Gadzos have established.

Objects

Among all the objects existing in the world, there are some belonging to the dead. To destroy them, that is, to subtract them from the whole, brings about an awareness of this whole. To not destroy all so as to preserve a few that can then only be used with precaution makes manifest the particularity of some elements and the homogeneity of all the rest. To attribute no distinctive sign to these objects, letting them circulate freely, even though they have to be handled in a particular manner, amounts to creating the possibility for particularity to appear unexpectedly under any given circumstance, this even while limiting its perception to only a few people aware of its possible existence. It also amounts to inviting these few people to permanently practice observation and interpretation: anything can be endowed with a particular status, that of *mullo*.

This process does indeed appear to be aimed at bringing about the perception of both particularity and totality even while attributing to each a different quality (value, status). This does not occur by setting them into opposition but, on the contrary, by showing how one is inscribed into the other.

The "Things of the World" the Dead Used to Like

Pulling out a few items from all the foods, all the things circulating in the world that are pleasing to human beings, makes people aware of the rest. When for instance a dish, a food, a song, or an activity that had been taken out of the movement of life is put back into circulation, it acquires a new status: it is not something given by the world but something that the living individual concerned puts into the world. The fact that there is no distinctive sign appended to it, that there is no talk about

what is going on, and, at the same time, that anything could be charged
with this particular quality, leads to the idea that the person following this
practice has thus been made capable of conceiving the totality of things.

Time

In the case of time, the mode of appropriation is less specific and also
more complex. In a time that is not an undifferentiated space but one already cut up and punctuated by the rhythm of the calendar and by the
activities of Gadzos, the Mānuš inscribe their particularity in two ways.
(1) They set up disturbances [*décalages*] [12] in their adherence to the
rhythm of the Gadzo calendar: they celebrate certain holidays and not
others, they invent their own (birthdays, deaths . . .) and insert qualitative gaps (periods of mourning). (2) They invent durations, notably
some defined by individually determined and perceived attitudes to the
name and memory of the dead. Two such types of durations emerge
when looking at what happens to the memory and the name of the dead.

One duration is made up of the ephemeral, the precarious, the irremediable (or rather the feeling of the ephemeral, of precariousness, of
the irremediable . . .). It is felt with the affirmation of the unique character of each individual and the events he or she has lived through, a
character manifested for instance by refusing any inheritance (of wealth
and of names) and choosing instead to destroy the deceased's property.

The other duration pertains to the perennial, the immutable (the feeling of . . .). It is felt through the absolute loyalty to the deceased, in the
silence surrounding the dead, a silence that is not a forgetting or that only
becomes a forgetting when the presence of the dead among the living is
ensured. Silence appears at once as the most accomplished image of this
forgetting and as an infallible memory. Forgetting and memory coincide.

These two durations (or rather the feeling of their existence) are established through the mediation of the dead. The durations might appear contradictory, as they involve, on the one hand, the elimination of
historical memory and the disappearance of individual singularity, a disappearance accompanied by the affirmation of the irreplaceable nature
of this singularity, and, on the other hand, the advent of the immutable
presence of the anonymous Mānuš ancestor. The relationships maintained by these two durations offer an image of the relation between the
group and the individual within the community—the ephemeral individ-

ual in the guise of Nīni, Garçounet, Piroto, etc., who are nonetheless immutable insofar as they are Mānuš. At the same time, the relationship of these two durations offers an image of the Mānuš–Gadzo relation, each of their encounters confirming that Gadzos keep on behaving like Gadzos and expect the Mānuš, be they basket makers or iron workers, nomads or sedentary, to keep on behaving like tramps.

Space

Space is put through a process similar to that of time. Mānuš conform to the spatial organization imposed by the Gadzos, limiting themselves to marking it only in some spots with their presence, notably in the cemetery, and this in a way that, though not specific to them, is at least spectacular (though they are not themselves the instigators of visibility). But space is dealt with in the same way as the objects and the things of this world the dead favored. The Mānuš take some sites out of current usage, that is, from usage as defined by the Gadzos. These are the *mūlengre placi* and all places marked by Mānuš death. Thus the totality of space as a whole-organized-by-the-Gadzos becomes perceptible. Nothing distinguishes these places as particular (except that usually there's nobody in them—I do find interesting that the places inscribing Mānuš presence in the universe are places with no one in them), and theoretically any site might be such a place, even when practical considerations make this difficult. These "places" can be the locus of events whose meaning can only be understood by the Mānuš (such as a trailer turned around or pelted, or other such unexplained incidents . . .), as only they are aware that these events call for interpretation.

The Advent of Meaning

The process whereby objects that belonged to the dead are burned or made to disappear, whereby the departed's name is no longer uttered and her or his memory no longer evoked, does indeed establish a void or the appearance of a void. But at the same time it gives voice to that which is disappearing, a voice that, at the very moment of its disappearance, says something (Garçounet is dead), a something which establishes a durable affirmation (we are Mānuš—Garçounet in the guise of a defunct makes us Mānuš). How can that which is disappearing be made to say something? Precisely by not making everything disappear and by leaving in use that which has been preserved but which has now been given the same status as that which has disappeared, namely that of *mullo*. Meaning emerges from the play of emptiness and fullness (or fullness turned into emptiness and emptiness that is known to be full). This emergence of meaning is the advent of the Mānuš in the world of the Gadzos.

The introduction of gaps [*décalages*] in the midst of a totality, the assignment of differential values to the resulting elements, and the drawing of meaning from their confrontation is a well-known process. Roman Jakobson has argued that this is the way meaning appears in language (Jakobson 1976). Thus, this process is not specific to the emergence of Mānuš meaning, that is, to the emergence of the Mānuš world itself.

But particularity is present in the way that has been chosen to make this emergence of meaning possible, that is, in the gestures and the attitudes I have described. Anthropologists see the sorts of situations where the dead help in constituting the living into a unique group as very common and have labeled them rites of passage. However, up to now I have avoided using words such as "rite" and "ritual," even though I do think that Mānuš gestures toward their dead are rites. In terms of a limited definition of rites, they do establish a relationship between instances that don't belong to the same dimension (such as the visible and the invisible), they bring about a transformation in the course of life, and they are obligations to those who perform them. And yet some of the aspects of Mānuš rites do not seem to quite conform to most ethnographic descriptions of "rites." Their specificity, however, is constructed not so much through one aspect or another but through the accretion of several of these.

Mānuš rites are not public. There is no announcement, no indication that someone is performing a rite by refusing to eat a given dish or by taking care of one dog more than others. And yet, neither are they secret. It can happen that the fact of the "rite" being public or not is of no concern. The bereaved might witness the departed's car go up in flames, but they might just as well bring the car to a junkyard to be demolished and leave without waiting to see it happen.

These gestures are not collective either. During funerals, which are the only occasions when there are gatherings, nothing happens except that the Mānuš show, both to themselves and to the Gadzos, that they are assembled. Likewise, acts of homage to the graves are aimed at insuring the image of the united group. Each individual does perform those rites but without broadcasting it.

Mānuš rites are permanent (which seems paradoxical for "rites of passage"). There are always some dead in need of respect and visits. There are always some Mānuš among the living in the process of paying homage to their dead and thus producing gestures calling for interpretation. And even if no one is doing this at a given moment, the discreet character of the acts of homage, the innocuous nature of the gestures through which they are performed, the ordinary aspect of the objects on which they are practiced, make for a situation where everyone must always act as if there were something to be interpreted. *Mulle* objects are everywhere.

Mānuš rites allow individual initiative (in the choice of the objects targeted for ritual acts, the choice of the gestures to be performed, such as destruction or preservation, the choice of duration . . .), and because of this they are only imperfectly standardized. They thus leave room for uncertainty. Nothing embodies ritual references, such as a book or a specialized body of, for instance, priests or judges, or even elders (there are so few old people in this community), from which all concerned could seek the truth of the rites. In spite of all their variations, all these gestures partake of the same goal: to successfully insure the coexistence of the living and the dead. And even though these rites are not accompanied at the moment of their performance by any words, any commentary, all the Mānuš, when asked, claim they are necessary, and they give the same explanation for this necessity: respect.

THESE RITUAL PROPERTIES are not the result of chance. I will first look at some of their consequences. They turn the perception of meaning into a perpetual questioning. Any object can be a marked object since there is no sure sign that can distinguish it. And the silence that surrounds all action makes for constant striving toward interpretation. But the necessity of interpretation doesn't plunge the Mānuš into anxiety or perplexity: people who are aware that meaning is everywhere and that it can appear at any moment also know which gestures they are required to perform when meaning does appear: they are the gestures of "respect."

There is a concrete illustration of such a relationship with meaning in a specific domain of the communication between the living. It pertains to *cajxi*, "signs, traces," which Joseph Valet's *Vocabulaire* ([1971] 1986) felicitously translates as "signs on the road,"[13] which were commonly created at the time of horse-drawn trailers. *Cajxi* form an ensemble of signs the nature of which is more akin to a hermeneutic than a code. The first requirement Mānuš have for these signs is that they should not look like signs. Gadzos must not notice them. Thus such a sign could be a tuft of grass covered with a few pebbles at a crossroad, a small pile of sand or dirt in the middle of a path, a fragment of rag attached to a hedge or a low branch, or even an empty pack of cigarettes crumpled up on a pile of gravel abandoned by road workers on the side of a road, and so forth. People who know how to read such signs can find a meaning in that which must appear to have none. They are only seen by those who know that there must be signs. Yet, there is always some doubt about their nature: this grass and this gravel scattered at the side of the road, this bit of dirt flattened up in the middle of the road, this rag tossed about by the wind . . . are they really there to say something? Mānuš signs always repeat the same message: we passed through here. There is another Mānuš word that reveals there is no difference in nature between the objects of the dead and signs on the road. I cite again Joseph Valet: "*niš:* keepsake of a defunct or sign of passage, piece of wicker attached to the car, to the shafts of a horse drawn trailer—, *is man i niš ke mur prāl dejas man,* 'I had a keepsake my brother had given me.'" *Niš:* trace of a passage / trace of a presence. If my brother is alive, I know he passed through here, I know he and I are in touch. If my brother is dead, he did pass, I don't see him but I still know he and I are in touch. *Niš* is also the wicker attached to the car. The living and the dead are linked like the wicker to the steel of the shaft. But the mediation of the dead, as it links the living to each other, also isolates them from one and other.

To Isolate

Mānuš rites have an individual dimension. People do not explain their behavior, and no questions are asked. Respecting the dead also involves respecting the silence of the living, as it could always be a silence of "respect" for the dead. This silence, perhaps stemming from the peace that comes between oneself and one's dead, envelops individuals and fami-

lies. They each have the guarantee that if they do what is required with
their dead, they are fully Mānuš, and that's enough. The contrast between the place held respectively by the loyalty to the dead and the concern with one's reputation among the living among these Mānuš and
other Gypsy groups is striking (I am thinking for instance of the Kalderaš Rom [Williams 1984]).

To Link

Mānuš assess how close other Gypsy groups are to them primarily on
the basis of the respect they give their dead. They assess the behavior of
individuals within their own community the same way. And since, on the
one hand, respect for the dead prevents the asking of direct questions,
and, on the other, individuals will not comment on their own actions, all
the members of the group are in a constant state of mutual observation.
There are two ways of shedding light on the behavior of other people:
interpretation and gossip, the latter thus involving reliance on third
parties. We can see at this point that the silence brought by the dead ac-
tivates communication among the living (just as we had seen that de-
stroying the possessions and spending the money of the defunct acti-
vated solidarity). Both solutions involve risk: that of being blamed for
one's curiosity when having recourse to a third party, or that of making
an error in the case of interpretation. Communication is always fraught
with danger. But in these two cases the risk is reduced because curiosity
is universal and people are usually pretty much familiar with the context
and thus able to correctly interpret each other's actions. One evening, a
young man, Pēpe, picked a fight with a mature man, Xitāri, known to be
particularly vindictive. Voices were raised and threats uttered, and suddenly Pēpe rushed into his trailer and came out with a rifle. Xitāri hesi-
tated a moment, and stopped yelling; it seemed he was about to throw
himself on his adversary, but then he suddenly turned away and left. The
fight abruptly came to an end. The next day Xitāri explained to me that
the rifle was *i mulli puška,* "a dead person's rifle," belonging to Pēpe's father, deceased two years earlier. He had not wanted to insult the rifle of
a dead man. Of course he only had to explain this to me, as everyone
else had understood why he turned away. They all knew the context and
did not think that Xitāri was afraid of confronting Pēpe.

(An anecdote: courtship exposes people to the same dangers. Conversation between a boy and a girl is frowned upon, so there only remains interpretation: looks, attitudes, or calling upon a third party to deliver messages. With the same means are associated the same risks: mistakes and blame.)

THREE

Civilizing the World

In the next two chapters I will revisit the circumstances and attitudes I have just described, in order to look at them at another level, that of "the Mānuš among the Gadzos," the implications of which I have not yet brought to light. At this level, there is a temptation to see specific traits in terms of adaptation. After all, it is hard to overlook the fact that Mānuš affirmation has to occur in the midst of another society, and thus there cannot fail to be some correlations between the nature of this society and the nature of this affirmation, or, more precisely, between the nature of the latter and the fact that it is expressed within a world defined by others. But I don't think that these correlations can be limited to a deterministic interpretation. The way to avoid this oversimplification is by first looking at the immersion of the Mānuš in the Gadzo world.

The statement "the Mānuš live in the world of the Gadzos" rather than only "in the same world as the Gadzos" might seem surprising in that it amounts to claiming, for instance, that the Mānuš have no direct relationship to nature, since such a relationship has to be always mediated by the Gadzos . . . Are Mānuš not *Hekišlup,* "bush people," "making their nest in the bushes"? Have I not evoked their fondness for camping in the countryside, their skills at hunting and fishing, their thorough knowledge of the flora and fauna of this region? It is a surprising statement in that it implies, when we give more thought to it, that the Mānuš, after having coexisted or while coexisting with the Gadzos, are detaching themselves from them, are putting themselves at a distance, which precisely causes them to become Mānuš and the Gadzos to become Gadzo.

The universe in which the Mānuš travel is entirely filled with markers. Gadzos are already everywhere the Mānuš can go. The roads and paths they are traveling on have been built by Gadzos; the places where they are camping have been delimited by Gadzos (these places are today referred to as "designated" and "regulated" for use by the *Gens du Voyage* ["Travel People"][1]); the fields and woods they are exploring have been fenced, planted, cultivated by the Gadzos who guard them. But the Mānuš have the ability to appropriate all of this. Not as competitors of the Gadzo conquest, exploitation, and transformation of nature, but in the ways and modes specific to them and which Gadzos do not understand. The dead act as the main, though not the sole, operator in this appropriation.

MY DESCRIPTION OF THE MODES of constitution of meaning, that is, of the advent of the Mānuš through the establishment of all things *mulle,* allows us to make out two phases. The first phase is one in which the act of withdrawing something from the world (an object, a food, an activity, a locale . . .) enables the totality to appear. This specific operation reveals the cultural character of this totality. And what thus comes to light is indeed total Gadzo mediation between the Mānuš and nature. In the second phase, something that had been made to disappear is made to reappear (the person who had renounced the use of something puts it back into use); the totality is then given back to homogeneity—it is, in a manner of speaking, voided and turned again into a simple environment.

Those who have stopped drinking wine or eating a special dish of hedgehog, rabbit, etc., or singing a song because of the death of one of their loved ones are actually civilizing the wine, the dish of hedgehog or rabbit, the song . . . through their renunciation. When they begin to drink, eat, or sing again, all this no longer represents foods, dishes, ordinary endeavors, or simple products of nature or of the Gadzos, but rather a ritual transformation through which those who renounced are now nourishing themselves from Mānuš civilization.

This civilizing ability that Mānuš society offers each of its individual members is limitless. As I noted, it can act upon anything circulating in the world. And it is tested by the fact that one who performs these gestures is free to stop performing them at any time, an individual decision that need not be disclosed to anyone. One who renounces is also free to decide against putting these things back into circulation. We thus encounter individuals bereft of wine, or game meat, or fowl, or bereft of cognac or of plum brandy, bereft of trout fishing, or of guitar . . . Out of everyone else, they are the ones who possess these things most fully. Abstinence can thus be the supreme form of possession. In this respect, it might be remembered that when I described the trajectory followed by a departed's evocation, I wrote that silence and then forgetting were the fullest forms of "respect," of faithfulness to the dead, that is, to memory.

The Mānuš are better hunters than the Gadzos because they are more civilized than the latter and not because they are more "natural," closer to nature, an impression others who see them as "bush people" have of them. The separation of civilization from barbarism is based on the respect for the dead. Mānuš are reminded of this by the story of the Mānuš, the Pirdo (Traveler), and the hedgehog.

The Story of the Mānuš, the Pirdo, and the Hedgehog

Moršela told this story on a summer day of 1982 during a break in a game of *pétanque* he was playing with his cousin and me on the fairground of a village in the *département* of Creuse. We had gone to the café to drink some wine. As we were getting up to resume our game, Moršela said: "*Tiens, žānen gar o phenas mange vavax mōlo u Tchāvolo? . . .*," "By the way, do you know what the Tchāvolo told me the other day? . . . ," and he told us the story of the Mānuš, the Pirdo, and the hedgehog (a few days later I took advantage of the arrival of Moršela's father-in-law to ask him to repeat the story and to record it).[2]

*Mur phrāl i . . . U Tchāvolo, mur phrāl. Brinžen les teme. U Tchāvolo. Jop krelo kīrbi eškane. Njale krelo kīrbi, i les **un tir** žāne. **Bon,** is ap i placa mit kāla kirbāria. Vartrens le u kīrbo. Ap u **champ de foire,** an u gap. Maškral u gap, čele kampini koj ap u **champ de foire.** Pur u kīrbo mukenle . . . Ako dives vias ko Pirdo, k o kirbāri paš leste, paš mur phrāl, u Tchāvolo . . . Brinže les ku rom, **le Gros Tatav!** . . . U thūlo, krelo jop nina kīrbi . . . Ako dives vias paš u Tchāvolo te žanle niglenge. Te lel les u Tchāvolo mit niglenge! Kek žūkel is paš ko Xulio, ko Tatav. Ako dīves paš u Tchāvolo: "**Allez mon frère, on va aux hérissons! Allez mon frère, on va aux hérissons!**" Xajas peslo ap leste! U Tchāvolo kamels gar. "**Non,** phenelo, žō gar. Un našti gar te mukap tuke mur tin žūkli ke žāli gar mit vavax. Te žāla tuva, našeli, rodeli gar un našrel pesli! Me žō gar! . . . So but šafrepen i man!" . . . Kamels gar te žālo u Tchāvolo, xoxelo, ajve?*

Mais tellement ke xajas peslo ko Pirdo ap leste: *"Allez,* ǧā
menge!," phenel u Tchāvolo. K ako dives, ako dives is leste! Viaso
dinelo ko . . . mur phrāl . . . ǧāne leste i *frigidaire* leste. An leskri
kampina, *frigidaire* i les, ku Tatav. Kote dren čelo u nīgle. Mangel
te venle raziremen u nīgle, pucede ajve? Un čivel le lo dren! ǧānō
gar me kiči mukel le kote dren, an ko bedo . . . šila . . . u *frigidaire*
i . . . *peut-être deux trois jours* mukel le dren, otax, ǧānō gar me,
sept huit jours mukel le dren! Fuj! . . . Xal le kake! Un ǧāne ax
xal kāva! Oh Je! *Eh ben* te dikes te xal glan tute ko peso, *eh ben*
butdax kek bok ap tute!

Viaso paš u Tchāvolo. Xajaspeslo. Hals! *"Allez mon frère, on
va rodav des nigle! Allez mon frère! Allez mon frère!* . . ."

Akele an i viza! U Tchāvolo lias peskri tin ǧūkli, mukas la lōs,
ǧanle kake, u Tchāvolo rodelo gar jop, phenelo či pur i tin ǧūkli. Ki
ǧūkli, ǧāne la? fun u Tchāvolo, i Lūbli . . . Niglenge ki ǧūkli, i kek!

Allez, krenle jek felda, vavax felda, vavax . . . dikenle či, acen
le či. U Tchāvolo mukel, dikel o krelo ko Xulio, rodelo gar jop,
un u vavax, kāva, krelo ke rodel, pur xaxeste, ǧānelo gar te rodel
nīgle . . . *Allez!* Vavax heko, vavax heko . . . Kane risenle pal ko
heko, akelo ko nīglo glan lende! Nīglo an i grāza. Kake! Nīglo!
Oh! Šūkar! Dikelo les u peso, u Kirbāri. Dikelo. Un glan ko
nīglo, vavax nīglo i! Un glan kāva, vavax nīglo papse! U papse
jek glan! Nox . . . papse jek! . . . Ova, kake i, phenelo mange u
Tchāvolo, jek šel nīgle kake jek palan i vavax . . . Oh! U Thūlo
Tatav, so frō ilo! Lel peskro gono. *Allez!* Krelo pre ko gono, so
frō! U pāni vial leskre krat an u muj! Ajve? *Mais au moment* kaj
čivelo ko Pirdo u vast ap o nīglo, u eršto nīglo, u nīglo risel pes lo
pale, un phenel leskre . . . phenelo ko nīglo pur u peso, valštikes
phenelo: *"Eh ben mon frère! Tu vois pas qu'on est en train d'-
suivre le convoi d'mon pauv'père?"*

It's about my brother . . . My brother, the Tchāvolo. You know
him. The Tchāvolo. Now he works carnivals. He works them in the
summer, he has a carny booth, you know. So, he was at a place
with these "carnies." He was waiting for the carnival to start. On
the fairgrounds, in a village. In the middle of the village, all these
trailers were on the fairgrounds. They are allowed for the carnival
. . . Every day, this Traveler, this "carny," came to see him, he was
coming to see my brother, the Tchāvolo . . . You know that guy, Fat

Tatav, he does carnivals too . . . Every day he came to get my brother to go with him to hunt hedgehogs, to get him to come hunt hedgehogs with him. This Tatav, this "métis," didn't have a dog. He was there every day, calling Tchāvolo: "Come, my brother, let's go hunt hedgehogs! Come, my brother, let's go hunt hedge-hogs!" He was eating [bugging] him. The Tchāvolo did not want to go. "No, he kept on saying, I'm not going. And I don't want to lend you my bitch because she won't hunt with anyone but me. If you take her, she'll run away, she won't hunt and she'll just run away! No, I'm not going! I have too much work!" He didn't want to go, the Tchāvolo, he was lying, you see?

But this Traveler was eating him so much. "Alright, let's go!" said Tchāvolo. Because every day, every day he was there! Eating him! My brother was going nuts . . . You know this Tatav has a fridge, he has a fridge right in his trailer. That's were he puts the hedgehogs. He asks someone to shave them for him, to clean them up, you see? And he puts them in there! I don't know how long he puts them in that thing! It's cold . . . a fridge . . . He leaves them there perhaps two, three days, or I don't know, perhaps even seven, eight days . . . Disgusting! He eats them that way! And you know how he eats them! Oh Jesus! If you saw him eating, that fatso, in front of you, you'd lose your appetite."

He was coming to get my brother. He was eating him. All the time! "Come, my brother, let's go *rodav des nīgle!* Come, my brother! Come, my brother!"

So here they are in the fields! The Tchāvolo had taken his little dog along, he had taken off its leash. They are walking this way, the Tchāvolo isn't searching, he says nothing to his little dog. You know that dog, the Tchāvolo's dog, Lūbli. There's no better dog to hunt hedgehogs!

So they "do" a hedge, another hedge, and another . . . They see nothing, they find nothing. The Tchāvolo doesn't care. He is keep-ing an eye on this "métis," he himself is not searching and the other is just pretending to search, it's just pretend, he doesn't know how to look for hedgehogs . . . So another bush, and another . . . Right at the moment they get to the other side of this bush there's the hedgehog, right under their feet! A hedgehog in the grass. Just like that! A hedgehog! Oh what a beautiful hedgehog! The fat carny sees it. He looks, and in front of that hedgehog

there's another! And in front of that one yet another! And then
another in front! And another and another! . . . Yes, the Tchāvolo
told me that's the way it was, about one hundred hedgehogs one
behind the other . . . Oh! Fat Tatav is so happy! He grabs his sack.
He opens his sack, he's so happy! His mouth is already watering!
You see? But at the moment he's about to grab the hedgehog, yes
this Traveler, his hand on the first hedgehog, the hedgehog turns
around and says to him . . . The hedgehog says to Fatso in French:
"Hey, my brother! Can't you see that we are following the funeral
of my poor father?"

Once he was through recording the story, Moršela asked me not to
let *menši fun kate*, "Mānuš from here," and particularly not Fat Tatav,
hear it. As to the others, *kre dox o kame!* "do what you want!" When I
asked Tchāvolo if the story was true, he smiled and, shaking his head as
someone in the know, said in French, "Ah yes! It's my brother Moršela
who tells this story!" and made no other comments.

MORŠELA IS A MĀNUŠ and the youngest of five siblings. His mother's
side of the family was descended from one of the German families that
arrived in France in the second half of the nineteenth century. His father's side of the family was sometimes referred to as Spanish Mānuš by
the German ones, as they spent a short time in Spain between the two
world wars. Moršela's parents were stuck in a hamlet of Creuse during
the second world war. Moršela was born in 1945 in this *département.*
Since then, with the exception of a few short stints of grape picking at
harvest times in the Bordelais region and around Bergerac, the area of
circulation of his family has been limited to Creuse and some communes
in neighboring *départements.* All the brothers, however, remained nomadic. At the end of the fifties, they traded in their horse-drawn wagons
for modern trailers (*camping*[3]) pulled by a car or truck. Only the widowed mother along with a son who remained single kept a horse-drawn
wagon. Like most of his relatives in the area, Moršela usually camps in
villages or small burgs, preferably away from houses. Even though the
Mānuš are well known in the region, they are still regularly expelled
from the places they stay, as most of the communes limit or completely
forbid (which is illegal) the camping of nomads on their territory. How-

ever, even when he is not harassed by the authorities, Moršela seldom stays anywhere for more than a week. He is forced to change his habits in winter, which is harsh here, when Moršela and his brothers rent a piece of land where they can spend the three worst months, from December to March. Moršela's family's everyday language is Mānuš. At the time he was telling this story, Moršela was married and the father of six children. When speaking about himself, Moršela simply says he is a Mānuš, and if I ask him to be more precise, he answers *Ext Mānuš,* "a real Mānuš," or even (with a bit of provocation—as he does have a dark skin), *Kālo Mānuš,* "Black Mānuš."

Tchāvolo is Moršela's older brother. At that time, in 1982, he was fifty-six years old and the father of twelve children. His life differed little from that of Moršela, except that, a few years earlier, he had become a "carny" in addition to his numerous activities. He had bought a stand, a *métier* [a trade, a profession], that is, a small balloon-shooting stand (with five air rifles), and, from April to September, he followed the carnival circuit in the *départements* of Creuse and Corrèze. This brought him into a new travel rhythm which involved regularly spending one week in each village and stopping in new places in the midst of the houses, such as a street or the main square. He had made new acquaintances from among the other carnival people, some who call themselves Mānuš or Sinte but no longer speaking any Gypsy language, and others who call themselves *Voyageurs* [Travelers] and, like the first two groups, speak a French argot mixed with some words of Gypsy origin. Finally, some are Gadzos and go to some lengths not to be confused with the others. Tchāvolo also had come to be exposed to new attitudes: that of the carnival people used to stopping in full view of local population. They benefit from the tolerance of the authorities and can enjoy the same tranquility week after week, in contrast to the Mānuš camping in the bushes and constantly suspect in the eyes of the authorities, who kept on threatening to expel them. During the whole of the carnival circuit time, Tchāvolo was separated from his brothers. They did, however, meet in the course of travel for work or pleasure. "Carnies" have tendency to avoid the company of the "bush people," whom they accuse of giving a bad image to Travelers. They readily claim that Mānuš are "savages" or "backward." Moršela was well aware of these prejudices,

and it was typical that when finding Tchāvolo in the company of carnival people, he adopted a provoking attitude: he only spoke Romani to
his brother, and this preferably in public places such as cafés, even while
fully knowing that the carnies couldn't understand him and were irri-
tated by this show of exoticism.

Fat Tatav, a carny by profession,[4] made his appearance each year in
the region during the holiday season. He owned two *métiers:* a shooting
stand and a carousel for children. He was indeed very corpulent, and it
is true that he owned a truck and a big trailer with a refrigerator inside.
It is also true that he kept hedgehogs in this "fridge," hedgehogs that
some of his colleagues including Tchāvolo cleaned up for him. To Gadzos, he presented himself as a professional carny, while he called himself
a Traveler when dealing with the carnies and the Mānuš. I heard him
claim at times that he belonged to a family of Sinti from Piedmont. He
did not speak Romani but the Travelers' argot.[5]

Moršela, Tchāvolo, and all their Mānuš kin in the area are accomplished hunters and love to eat hedgehog. These mammals are abundant
in this landscape of bushes, fields, and hedges. Moršela, Tchāvolo, and
their cousins practice different seasonal hunting techniques, as hedgehogs hibernate in their nests in winter and run around the countryside
in summer. Mānuš never take a female of childbearing age nor one they
find with her young. They have explored their territory so well that they
know exactly which hedge is home to a great number of hedgehogs. At
times they decide against hunting in such a place during a certain period
(in the fall for instance) so as to let the number of animals grow or to
save this spot for the time when hunting is difficult elsewhere (when
snow is falling, for instance). Likewise, they have various recipes tailored
to the physiological state of the hedgehogs, which changes with the seasons: braised in the winter, when the animals have their winter fat, and
boiled down into aspic with strong flavors (garlic, peppers, thyme, bay
leaves) in the summer, when hedgehogs run all night long and their meat
is smelly. Hedgehogs are not killed ahead of time but just before eating.
Sometimes when a hunt has been particularly successful the captured
hedgehogs are kept alive for a few days, in a big metal can, an empty bar-
rel, or a container made up of tires piled on top of each other. Regardless of the recipes used, the technique for butchering them is always the
same, and for Mānuš there is only one proper way of accomplishing this

task. It has to be done outside and a fire must be lit. Only a stick and a knife are necessary.

Many authors have noted similarities between hedgehogs and their favorite eaters. Judith Okely, writing about the Traveller-Gypsies of Great Britain, notes:

> [The hedgehog] lives on the fringes of the wild, or to be more exact, in shrubs and hedges, neither in open fields, nor in the thick of woods. Like the Gypsy, it lives in liminal areas, the very boundaries which demarcate a Gorgio's property. Another term for the "*hotchiwitchi*" is "*pal*" of the "*bor,*" "brother of the hedge." Gypsies select those traits with which they most identify. (Okely 1983, 101–2)

The hedgehog holds a large place in the conversations of Moršela, Tchāvolo, and all those Mānuš who camp near bushes. They talk about their hunts, compare recipes, or simply enjoy evoking the figure of the *nīglo*. They praise its ability to go everywhere, they appreciate its cleverness and its gluttony (it sneaks into vegetable gardens, it pigs out so much during apple season that its flesh tastes of apple . . .), they joke about its amorous exploits, they admire its bravery (it isn't afraid of snakes). These stories clearly show that there is a sense of complicity, that the Mānuš wish to see complicity between themselves and the hedgehog. One of Moršela's cousins, Dorine, narrates a tale he is fond of and which evidences such identification:

> . . . *Viaso phūro ko nīglo. Phūro nīglo! phenelo: "**Bof**, o krō me kate an ku heko? Kaj te mangap te xap? Kek menšo! Oba, phenelo, ǯāvo fort! ǯīvo mur ǯīben kake, ǯāvo man kaj meneste pur te ǯal mur ǯīben! . . ."*
>
> . . . He had become old, this hedgehog. An old hedgehog! He said: "Well, what am I doing in this bush? Where can I ask for something to eat? Not from a relative! Yes, he says, I'm going away! I'm going to live my life, I'm going somewhere to live my life! . . ."

Like Moršela and Tchāvolo, all Mānuš own one or more dogs. These are small dogs of a terrier or fox terrier type, trained to track animals, mainly hedgehogs, in the bushes. They adapt to the different modes of hunting, searching in the bushes in winter and following the scent in the grass in summer. Often bitches are called Lūbli, "whore."

THE STORY OF THE MĀNUŠ, the Pirdo, and the hedgehog reaffirms the
definition of Mānuš identity. This reminder is linked to the circumstance
of the narrator's brother's frequentation of carnies, Travelers or Pirde,
but in his story the reminder takes on the character of absolute truth.
The definition is not expressed as a maxim, it is offered to the listeners'
reflection, this through factors located at three levels: relations between
the living, relations between the dead and the living, and the relation between nature and culture.

The incredible aspects of the story—we don't know if we are dealing
with an account or a tale—make their appearances as so many invita-
tions to hermeneutic reflection. More than the gift of speech given to
animals, it is a clue for Mānuš, and only for Mānuš, that they should look
beyond the reported events. Moršela was telling this story in August,
and he claimed the events he described were very recent. The technique
of hunting he was describing, of walking in the fields while following a
dog which is supposed to discover the scent of a hedgehog, is a summer
technique, albeit a nighttime one. But it is never mentioned in the story
that the hunt was held at night. On the other hand, the narrator said that
"they 'do' a hedge, another hedge, and another" and yet, hedges are
"done" in winter, when hedgehogs are asleep in their nest in the midst
of the bushes.

Relations among the Living

The Pirdo Fat Tatav wants to behave as a Mānuš. Eating hedgehog seems
to him to be the Mānuš-making act. This seems to come out of the sort
of passion the bush people have for that animal. But Tatav is capable only
of eating hedgehog and doesn't know how to hunt or prepare it. He owns
a refrigerator but no dog. He only sees hedgehogs as meat and Mānuš as
hunters. But the hedgehog is a civilized being who respects its dead. It
is able to make this respect, that is, its civilized quality, be respected—its
hunt is not a wild roundup aimed only at satisfying appetites. The Mānuš
is a great hunter because he knows that he has to limit his harvest and
control his desires. From this knowledge and mastery stems his complicity with nature: the dog obeys only him. When Lūbli discovers the
hedgehog around a bush, the dog doesn't make the same mistake as the
Pirdo. The Mānuš, the hedgehog, and the dog understand each other
without the need for speech—and that is the Mānuš ideal. In contrast,

things must be explained to the Pirdo. We get the feeling from the start of the story that the Mānuš knows what's going to happen. He doesn't cause the Pirdo's confusion, he even seems to try to prevent it. But he ends up giving in to the Pirdo's endless demands. It's the Pirdo himself who is asking for the shame of being revealed as nothing but an ignorant barbarian, a stomach.

The Pirdo cannot be, doesn't know how to be, a Mānuš. This is what Moršela reminds everyone, and probably most of all his brother, who has taken to frequenting Pirde. And yet there does exist a risk of confusion, in that the Pirdo cannot be defined in a clear manner. To the Pirdo too there are Gadzos, and it cannot be said that he himself is a Gadzo. He might take up habits from the Mānuš lifestyle, by eating hedgehog, for instance. Or the Mānuš might adopt Pirde attitudes, which is what Tchāvolo was in the process of doing . . . This hesitation on how to define the Pirdo can be seen in the narrative. Fat Tatav receives multiple labels: *Pirdo* (which the Mānuš translate into French as *Voyageur* ["Traveler"]), *Xulio* ("métis"), *Rom* ("man"),[6] *Vavax* ("other"), *Tatav, Thūlo Tatav* ("Fat Tatav"), *Peso* ("fat"), and *Kirbāri* (the carnival person who owns and operates a carnival stand), also referred to by the French word *Fêtier*.[7]

Could we see the demonstratives (*ko xulio, ko Pirdo* . . .) that almost always come with these labels as markers of the distance the narrator seeks to establish? This comes out in that, while the definition of the Pirdo remains fuzzy, by the end of the story, the position he is assigned to is perfectly clear: he is not one of us. Fat Tatav, wanting to abolish the distance between himself and the Mānuš, addresses Tchāvolo as "my brother," and the story makes fun of this pretentiousness by having the hedgehog too address Tatav as "my brother," this time in a tone full of derision and commiseration for one who must irremediably remain on the outside.

It is of import that the opposition Mānuš–Pirdo is strikingly affirmed through one of the actions defining of the Mānuš (the capture and eating of hedgehog). The mentioning of gluttony seems to be a means usually used by these Mānuš to differentiate themselves from the people they encounter "on the road" (literally "on the voyage," *ap i rajza*) and with whom they could be confused. Here is another narrative, an account, this time, in which we find again the same hesitation along with

Here are the definitions in Joseph Valet's *Vocabulaire* (1971) for the terms with which the Mānuš refer to people they wish to establish distance from even though they cannot be viewed as Gadzos.

"*Sinto:* someone from Piedmont (Traveler), a foreign Mānuš. *Akele Sinte:* here come Travelers (different from us); *žūns o Sinte vejanle un sikranle beri un gajzi:* in the past, Piedmonters used to come and show [perform with] bears and goats."

"*Ungāri:* Hungarian, Rom Traveler. *Ungareca:* Hungarian woman. *Ungartikes:* in Hungarian. *O Ungaria raken ungartikes, ajvo gar but:* Hungarian Travelers speak in Hungarian (Romani), I don't understand much."

"*Španjolo:* Spaniard, a Spanish gypsy. *I Španjoli, bikrenle plaxti:* they are Spaniards, they are selling sheets."

"*Ralüš: raluche,* a pejorative term usually referring to the "Duville,"[8] they can be recognized by their accent and vocabulary."

"*Pirdo:* a non-Gypsy Traveler. *O Pirde žanle apo drom ar me, me i kek Mānuš un kek barengre, rakenle gar mānuš, grat ar Gāže ile:* Pirdes are on the road like we are, but they are neither Mānuš nor Yéniches, they don't speak Mānuš, they are just like peasants."

"*Bareskro: Yéniche* (pejorative term). *Bareskreca:* a *Yéniche* woman. *O Barengre i gar ar me:* The Yéniches are not like us."

"*Dandredo* (from *dandrova,* 'I bite,' *dandredo,* 'one who is bitten'): a non-Gadzo Traveler. *Kun i kāva? —Dandredo:* Who is it? —A Traveler. *I Dandredo i kāva:* he's a Traveler, that one."

"*Cirkāri:* circus people; *I Cirkārja kola:* those are circus people."

"*Kirbāri:* professional carny."

"*žamaskro:* a solitary Traveler, a tramp; *I žamaskro leskro gono apo trupo:* a 'tramp' with his backpack."

Xüilo: a non-Gypsy Traveler. *I Xüile kola, ajvenle gar romenes:* they are *Xüile,* they don't understand Mānuš."

the same clarity in the use of gluttony to establish distance. Tchāvolo is the narrator this time:

I mōlo vium Gouzon an. Viam Gouzon an. Un vias i tin sirka koj, ap i placa. žiam te dikhas i sirka u dīves. Rāti žiam fort niglenge . . . i duj žūkel k is man. Un u Kukeno is koj nīna paš mande ap i placa. žāne, njale, žiam fort niglenge. Acam šop, efta nīgle. Un ku Xulio, ku Sirkāri, xajsedo fun i bok islo! . . . Me žō pašo man. U Kukeno, u vavax, u tin Mānuš k is koj nīna ap i placa, un ko xulio, krenle brī jāg kote. Phenel ku vavax: "Ap! Marā le kal nīgle!"

These are Mānuš self-definitions in Valet:

"*Mānuš:* a Mānuš. *Mānušni* or *Mānušeca:* a Mānuš woman. *Am pardo Mānuš alojtre ketene:* we are lots of Mānuš altogether. *Rakō mānuš:* I speak Mānuš. *Tōde Mānuš:* former Travelers (literally: washed-out Travelers). *O tōde Māneš žanenle gar te rakenle mānuš:* 'washed-out Mānuš' don't know how to speak Mānuš."

"*Hajti:* nickname for Mānuš from Belgium. *Me ham Hajti, čače Māneš:* we are Hajti, true Mānuš."

"*Hesi:* a group of Mānuš who might have originated from Hesse and whose language is a bit different from the Auvergne Mānuš."

"*Šwobi:* Mānuš originating from Swabia."

"*Eftavagengre:* the people of the seven trailers. *I gili fun o Eftavagengre:* the song of the people of the seven trailers."

"*Gačkene Mānuš:* Mānuš originating from Germany as contrasted to the *Valštike Mānuš* (originating from France) and the *Prajstike Mānuš* of Alsace. *Rakenle gačkenes:* they are speaking in German."

"*Prajštiko:* Prussian, but also applied to a group of Alsatian Mānuš. *I Prajštiko Mānuš:* an Alsatian Mānuš."

"*Kiralengre:* cheese eaters (nickname of the Auvergne Mānuš)."

"*Hekišlup:* hedgehog hideout (nickname of the Mānuš who sleep under hedges); *Kāle Mānuš ke als an emligo them, i hekišlup:* these Mānuš who are always in the same area are *hekišlup.*"

"*Menšo:* man; *Me kamō gar te dikap o menši ke i gar mendar:* I don't want to see the man who is not one of ours. *Menši:* from the people near to us, Travelers; *I menši api placa:* there are Travelers on the square; *Livre menši:* good people looking for conversation (said when speaking of other Travelers)."

Valet adds some further definitions: "*Romenes:* in the manner of the Mānuš, in Mānuš language; *rakō romenes;* I speak in Mānuš. *Romnepen:* Mānuš language; *rakā o čačo romnepen:* we are speaking real Mānuš; *i ext romenes:* the true Mānuš language."

*U Kukeno fangela ān: "Na! Na! Na! žā karā sigedax u Tchā-volo!" žangen man le pre. Stō pre. Penō: "O kamena?" Is **au moins** dešenge, dešenge ti paš. Štum pre.*

*Ax umes pre, žum koj, brī jāg. Rajzam len kol nīgle. Pucuvam len un čivam len. U Kukeno žals te lel **au moins** deš litri mōja! . . . Ames koj. Xajam nīgle! Kram kol nīgle. Ku Xulio, ku tin Xulio xa-jas peske lo trin, jop zelbax kōkro! Trin nīgle! **C'est la vérité!** Trin nīgle xajaslo! U Kukeno štokels ap leste ke xālo! U vavax Mānuš*

*nīna! Me **jamais** dikum kake Mānuš otax xulio ke xal kake but*
nīgle! Penaso mange, trin nīgle krat te venle leskre an u muj ax či!
  *Deš nīgle **mais** panč nīgle xajaslo jop! Kanc bok!*
  *Pale pijam i slugo mōl. ǯiam pašas men is **au moins** dujenge.*
Ames štil.

Once I went to Gouzon. We arrived at Gouzon. And there was a small circus on the square. During the day, we went to see the circus. And at night we went hunting hedgehogs . . . With two dogs that I had. You now, summer, hunting hedgehogs; we found six, seven hedgehogs. And this métis, this Cirkāri, he was eaten by hunger! [he was starving!] . . . I went to sleep. The Kukeno and the other, the little Mānuš, who was also there on the square, and this métis, they made a big fire. The other said: "Come! Let's kill these hedgehogs!"

The Kukeno begins: "No! No! No! Let's first call the Tchāvolo!" They wake me up. I get up. I say: "What do you want?" It was at least ten, ten thirty . . . I got up.

Once I was up, I went there, by the big fire. We shaved these hedgehogs, we peeled[9] and cooked them. The Kukeno went to get at least ten liters of wine! . . . We remained there. We ate hedgehog. We prepared these hedgehogs. The métis, the little métis, he ate three hedgehogs all by himself! Three hedgehogs! That's the truth! He ate three hedgehogs! The Kukeno was astounded to see him eat! The other Mānuš also! I have never seen this, a Mānuš or a métis eating so much hedgehog! He told me that for him three hedgehogs, that's nothing at all! [literally: it's like nothing in his mouth!].

Ten hedgehogs, but he had eaten five of them! What an appetite!

After, we drank some wine. It was at least two in the morning when we went to bed. We were relaxed.

Relations between the Living and the Dead

The dead do not make an appearance in the story of the Mānuš, the Pirdo, and the hedgehog, but the living are sorted out in relation to them.

To say of someone that "he or she is eating his or her dead" is the worst possible insult. It does seem that this is what Moršela's story implies about Fat Tatav. But because it is a story and it has subtlety and poetic richness, the hint is stripped of its insulting characteristics. At any rate, a crude insult would have been not only gratuitous, as Fat Tatav wasn't present at the telling, but it would have also been a much poorer choice, as it wouldn't have been opened to interpretation and wouldn't have offered any explanatory principle. (My impression, each time I met Fat Tatav, is that he seemed debonair. In contrast to other professional carnies, he maintained good relations with the Mānuš, and my impression is that both Moršela and Tchāvolo felt kindly toward him. But in this narrative, it was necessary for the Pirdo character to be well known in order for the story to speak to the listeners and be edifying. Thus Tatav's ignorance and barbarism, which prevented him from being Mānuš, had to be emphasized. The reality of Fat Tatav had to be sacrificed to the efficacy of the message.)

We thus need to take into account the coherence of the three levels I have sought to separate. The first level enunciates a precept: one must differentiate oneself from the Pirde. The second level provides a justification for this precept: this has to be because the Pirde ignore the respect for the dead. The third level sets up the universe of values of which this precept partakes. I could also explain this interrelationship the following way: (1) The Pirdo is not a Mānuš. (2) This is the reason why the Pirdo is not a Mānuš. (3) This is what Mānuš are.

The Relationship of Nature and Culture

Moršela, Tchāvolo, Nīni . . . All these bush Mānuš who are the greatest hedgehog eaters in the world are not eating meat but are eating culture. In order to get rid of the innards, Moršela and his kin open hedgehogs "through the back." Opening a hedgehog through the back (the knife blade follows the spine by going under the bones, it goes from the coccyx to the head, the right and left sides of the animal are thus split apart without being detached from each other and so the hedgehog can be "opened" to clean out the innards) means that they belong to a specific family group; everyone knows that opening a hedgehog through the front means belonging to another Mānuš family group. The animal is then "dry" shaved; they hold a knife or a razor in their right hand and wedge the hedgehog under a foot while pulling on its hind legs with their left hand. Some Travelers pump up hedgehogs with a bicycle pump to make this process easier, but, to Mānuš, that would mean renouncing their Mānuš integrity. Moršela claims that he would certainly become ill if he were to eat a hedgehog that had been handled that way. The distinction between nature and culture is not a given, it is constructed, and it is indeed to this construction that Moršela's narrative refers. Anything can be nature, that is barbarism, if one is not able to control one's appetites. The refrigerator, the comfort of a modern trailer, and all the sophistication of urban areas mean nothing. Organic life triumphs in the person of Fat Tatav. At the same time, anything can be culture, that is civilization, provided one is capable of dominating the nature within. Respect for the dead is a double mastery of oneself and of the world.

The hedgehog knows the difference between the Mānuš and the Pirdo. When it speaks to the Pirdo, it doesn't hesitate between French and Mānuš. And the narrator has to specifically mention that the hedgehog is speaking French to the Pirdo, because in all likelihood the hedgehog's native language is Mānuš. So there is no need to evoke in the narrative, in reality, a privileged relationship of the Mānuš with animals, as there is only complicity between creatures that know how to bring about the transformation of nature into culture. In addition to his three dogs, Lūbli (like Tchāvolo's), Hafo, and Mickey, Moršela owns a crow, *Jacquot, u kurako.* Jacquot, whose wings have atrophied, freely wanders among the trailers and never gets lost. He can croak his name and faithfully every morning wakes Moršela up by imitating the crow of a rooster.

The message then is clear: we are civilized, our relation with the world is elaborated even in those actions that others only see as nature. A person who through ignorance would like to act as we do and might think he is like us would only succeed in making his barbarism evident. What is this knowledge? It is not knowledge that can be acquired, it is Mānuš identity itself. When I asked Moršela, Tchāvolo, or one of their cousins what makes a Mānuš (or why they are Mānuš), they all had the same answer: it's in the blood. A Mānuš is a Mānuš because he or she belongs to a Mānuš lineage, just as in the image of the hedgehogs lined up behind their ancestor, and a Mānuš is always so perfectly.

If a Mānuš hesitates or fails even a little bit to keep up this perfection, that person risks getting lost among all those people, *Xulie, Pirde,* carnies, Travelers, whose identities remain fuzzy. When Tchāvolo was following the carnival circuit, sometimes, when camping in the street of a small town, he was not able, didn't dare, to light a fire. He was then forced to dip the hedgehog he was preparing into a pot of boiling water to get rid of the quills that remained after shaving it with a knife. In contrast, when things are done "properly," the remaining quills should be burnt off on the flame and then scraped with a knife blade to produce a perfectly smooth rind. There is no difference between knowledge and blood: if Moršela were to eat a hedgehog prepared in a way different from the one practiced by his people, he would get sick. Culture runs in his veins.

Perhaps we can look upon that little tale told between two games of *pétanque* as a myth. It puts the deepest of questions into a relationship with the most ordinary experiences. And it does fit in with definitions of myth, even with those as far apart as Malinowski's notion of the myth as charter for society (Smith 1968, 527) and Lévi-Strauss's stance, according to which, in P. Smith's words, "myths are not only products of the mind but the privileged locus of the formation of categories. They not only serve to mark divisions already given in nature (as for instance man and woman, heaven and earth), but also introduce the discontinuity required for the work of the intellect by carving out gaps within continuity, as for instance nature and culture, us and them" (Smith 1968, 528) — and Mānuš and Pirde . . .

CIVILIZING THE WORLD

We cannot understand the modes of Mānuš affirmation without taking into account the saturated nature of the universe in which this affirmation is made.

The first gesture the Mānuš have to make so as to establish themselves is to create a breach in the coherence of Gadzo reality. They have to introduce discontinuity in it. In order to exist within a dense, filled-up universe, they have to establish a measure of void, of blankness, of absence . . . (at least that which is perceived as void, blankness, or absence in terms of Gadzo criteria, that is, in the terms of the people who are filling up the universe). The following is a concrete image of this process: it has to do with a *mūlengri placa* at the edge of a burg, on a main road. In the past Mānuš used to camp in that location at some distance from the village houses, and then someone died there. Over time, new dwellings came to be built by retired people who had returned to their native area or by the village tradespeople (these were pavilions, each with a garden, gravel pathway and flower beds, a garage halfway below the house, and an elevated front door reached by a short flight of stairs; the houses were uniformly painted beige or gray with white gables and geraniums in window boxes). So the place of the Mānuš dead became caught up in this line of pavilions. The empty lot (with no one staying there and an old trailer slowly rusting in it) appeared abandoned (weeds were growing on it and there was neither fence nor gate). And yet the family, made up of several brothers who were still frequenting the canton, disregarded both municipal injunctions and offers to buy the lot. I think the reason the family did in the end agree to sell was because a Mānuš piece of land had come to be standing out too spectacularly in the midst of Gadzo dwellings. Too much visibility is not appropriate for a *mūlengri placa*.

So this is the process of Mānuš appropriation: between the world and the Mānuš, there is the omnipresent Gadzo mediation (the fruits of nature and the works of the Gadzos are equivalent). In the uses they make of this nature-that-is-Gadzo-civilization, Mānuš introduce the mediation of the dead. The presence of the Gadzos is erased. But the Mānuš are not for that brought back to wild nature—they bathe in Mānuš civilization, they possess a kindred knowledge of everything that surrounds them.

The constitution of such fractures in the weave of the Gadzo universe represents the first stage in the nullification of the other. Moreover, the particular aspects of the Mānuš rituals I have described are not accidental. It is necessary that they be fragmented, uncertain, individual, silent, and private rather than regulated, unanimous, collective, imposed, and public. Mānuš affirmation isn't aimed at constituting a separate domain or an enclave but at appropriating the whole. In order for Mānuš civilization of the world to be total, it must not be public.

This is something Gadzos cannot perceive and understand. This misperception becomes part of Gadzo discourse, as evidenced for instance by the recent regulations aimed at Mānuš and at Gypsies in general. Officials, support organizations, and the media are asking them to say who they are, to "make themselves better known," to "speak up." But if the Mānuš undertaking were unanimous and public, it would be addressed to the Gadzos. The tombs, the only monuments that let the group be seen, do not say anything about how Mānuš things are, about what happens there. Rather, they are a silent presence, just like the crowd at funerals. So if the Mānuš undertaking were to be unanimous and public, its presence would no longer be inscribed within the Gadzo universe, it would be in opposition to it. If the Mānuš were to confront the Gadzos, the Mānuš wouldn't be able to nullify them. The relationship would lose its equivocal character. To have the capacity to nullify the Gadzos makes it possible to maintain all sorts of relationships with them, relations that can run the gamut from suspicious, familiar, or hostile, to solidarity or collaboration, and then again to competition or struggle, to avoidance, or exploitation (this in both directions: Gadzos exploiting Mānuš, Mānuš exploiting Gadzos). The relationship can also include admiration, disdain, indifference, or friendliness. Any systematization of the relation Gypsy–Gadzo, any typology of attitudes is challenged by a host of counterexamples. All these are played out within a fundamental withdrawal, but a withdrawal that is an actual taking possession of oneself.

The best word to use here might be "abstention" rather than "absence." Mānuš presence—undeniable, everyone knows they are here—doesn't speak, no one knows what to say of them. When Gadzos speak, they do not speak about the Mānuš but about "Gypsies," "bohemians," "nomads," "persons of nomadic origins," "the homeless."[10] Gadzos speak of other things, of their own phantasms, their categories, their problems; they speak of what they themselves have instituted. The advent of the Mānuš is accomplished by subtracting—by not consuming, not enunciating, not frequenting . . . This brings to mind my previous comments about the *mūlengre placi:* the places inscribing Mānuš presence in the universe are places with no one in them.

Here are some more illustrations of this in terms of space. Parallel to their ability to subtract certain places from Gadzo omnipotence/ omnipresence, the Mānuš also fill in spaces usually left temporarily vacant by the Gadzos. These are neglected or forgotten interstices within the Gadzo spatial grid, places that for us are empty (as made clear by the expressions designating them: wasteland, commons, *faux-chemins,*[11] abandoned roads, dumping grounds . . .) but which Mānuš take over, bringing in their things, their animals, their sounds, and all the meanings attached to them. But here too the relation is not unequivocal, it is modulated on a continuum spanning the taking over of forbidden public space and the acceptance of the *aires d'accueil,* areas specially set up by Gadzos for use by the *Gens du Voyage* ["Travel People"]. All this again to be understood within the Mānuš practice of a fundamental appropriation, their faculty of taking along Mānuš meanings and assigning them to everything.

In the domain of economic activities, there is the same positive practice toward that which the Gadzos perceive as empty. Here it is possible to evoke the skill with which the Mānuš slip into the interstices of the overall economy, integrating themselves into it without letting it swallow them up. For instance there is a parallel between what I said about the establishment of meaning and what can be observed in recycling activities, activities that are obviously not the sole purview of the Mānuš. (Mānuš modes of recycling are as follows: (1) We take note in the world, in the Gadzo world that is, of objects without value, "worthless." (2) We pick up these objects. (3) They become valuable again through the transformation we make them undergo or through the sole fact that they are assembled. (4) It's a value that benefits the Mānuš. We have thus made Mānuš life out of nothing.)

At this point I would like to bring up the stereotyped notion expressed in statements such as "these people don't do anything." Such utterances are met with well-intentioned automatic protests by the *Amis des Gens du Voyage* ["Friends of the Travel People"], who awkwardly claim that yes, like everyone else, Gypsies are working, except that we don't see them do so, they work at home, behind the trailers, or else they get up so early that when we get up they have already finished their workday, or again they are not working just now but they would work if they were given the opportunity, if someone would hire them . . .

Of course the Mānuš are working, but really, all those hours spent in cafés, in playing *pétanque* or quoit, in running around in the fields, searching through bushes? Yes, it is legitimate to describe these activities as leisure time, or as food gathering . . . But then there are all those hours spent in winter "by the fire" and in summer sitting on the grass, in the sun or in the shade, telling the same old jokes twenty times, twisting bits of reed into rings or whittling a twig till nothing remains of it, looking at the fire, teasing each other, playing with the children . . . All those times when an explicit invitation is made ("you'll come, right?"), and the guest does come, and sits down, and host and guest drink a bottle of wine, talk a little, and then they just sit around and nothing is happening. And then when the guest states he or she is about to leave: *vere tajsa?* ("you're coming tomorrow?"). All those "empty" hours in the face of the regulated, completely filled-up Gadzo time are again, by abstention, a retrenchment, a way of being in charge of one's own life. Because of course this "nothing" is all filled up with Mānuš intensity: the sounds, smells, presences, and voices—the whole world of the senses of a Mānuš encampment.

PERHAPS THE BEST ILLUSTRATION of the contrast between what the Gadzos are allowed to see and what is felt within the group can be found in Mānuš naming practices. Even though I am writing about the Mānuš of the Central Massif, I am drawing here in great part from an analysis done by Leonardo Piasere (1985, 209–21) on the Slovensko Roma he studied in the north of Italy.

An anecdote will help explain this. One day in September of 1982, I went to a café frequented by certain Mānuš families. The woman who owned the café said to me: "Did you hear? Fredo had an accident." The man named "Fredo"—Alfred L.—is called Garçounet among the Mānuš. I was with him a few minutes earlier and he was in perfect health. But he did tell me that two days earlier, three of his nephews were in a car accident. The café owner showed me the newspaper, and indeed, under the heading "Night and Day," it is announced that Messieurs Laurent, Alfred, and Baptiste L. were victims of a car accident and taken to the hospital.

Among "our" Mānuš everyone has two names, the *romeno lap,* or Mānuš name, and the "name for the Gadzos." Below is a chart showing the two types of names carried by the members of the L. family to which the café owner alluded. It explains the mix-up between the uncle and the nephew and brings to light the functioning of the naming system.

The chart lists only those individuals whom I mentioned in the anecdote. Actually, Moreno has eleven children—six boys and five girls. The uncles are godfathers to their nephews, and elder brothers are godfathers of the younger ones. As is the practice in France, they transmit

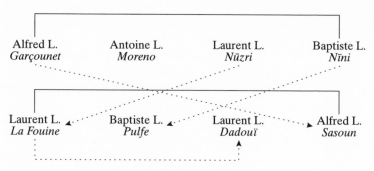

The dotted lines show relations of godparenthood.

their given names to their godsons: Garçounet baptized Sasoun, Nūzri baptized La Fouine, who in turn baptized Dadouï, while Nīni baptized Pulfe.

The "name for the Gadzos" conforms to Gadzo usage in the milieu in which the Mānuš live, that is, French usage. It is formed by a given name and a family name: Alfred L., Antoine L., Baptiste L., etc. It's the name used when dealing with Gadzos and on administrative documents. Mānuš do not use them in interactions within their community. Very often, these given names are not even known by some people, but there are rare cases when the given name serves as *romeno lap*. And yet, this given name, taken from the Christian calendar (until the arrival of Pentecostalism, Catholic priests officiated at baptisms), is transmitted from godfather to godson (from godmother to goddaughter), which leads to a great number of relatives having the same "name for the Gadzos" (here we have three Laurent L.'s and two Alfred L.'s), as it is the custom to choose godparents among blood kin. The "name for the Gadzos" is the name engraved on tombstones.

The *romeno lap* used within the community (though it is never a secret name) could be a nickname, a family name, an abbreviation, a given name, a regular noun (for instance the name of an animal, a flower, a color . . .), or an onomatopoeia. It is not transmitted. It ceases to be uttered by the family when the one who bore it dies. By way of illustration, here is a list of twenty female and male *romene lap* (the Mānuš simply say *i mur lap,* "it's my name"). I did not pick them. Instead, in order to provide an objective sample, I took three living generations of one family (in fact, the forty persons I mention do not make up the whole of the descendants of the original couple). Men: Pishoti, Garçounet, Moreno, Nūzri, Nīni, Šchtrackar, Tchāvo, Gūgi, Pipipe, Manuel, David, Tarzan, La Fouine, Dadouï, Pulfe, Jo, Sasoun, Tonio, David, Moïse . . . Women: Louisa, Fifille, Vejs, Pato, Poupée, Dondine, Pūpa, Ratié, Phajgue, Brigitte, Titite, Nita, Majkrits, Paulette, Rosita, Nenette, Bouguinette, Sabrina, Nado, Bluma . . . In Mānuš *tchāvo* means "boy," *štrackar,* "straight rod," *vejs,* "white," *pūpa,* "doll," *phajge,* "lily of the valley," *blūma,* "flower." There is also the Spanish *moreno,* "brown," and the French *la fouine,* "the marten." These are the only names in this list having a meaning. Parents usually "find" the *romeno lap* for their children (before that, the children are simply referred to as *u tchāvo* or *i čaj,* "the boy" or "the girl," or *u tikno, u tikno phrāl,* "the little one," "the little brother"). There is no naming ceremony. It can happen that this name changes in the course of childhood or adolescence (adults thus can have several *romene lap,* but only the current one is used and known by everybody). It can also happen that a nickname given by a person's age cohort supplants the name given by the parents (for instance, Starkie might replace Rīzo) or that a child's name is replaced by a man's name (Nudeli might become Vaillanto). If we were to look at a much larger sample of *romene lap,* we would have to conclude, like Leo Piasere does about the *romano imeno* of the Slovensko Roma, that the only regularity we can find in this stock of names is that of phonetic structure: consonant-vowel-consonant-vowel (CVCV or CVCVCV).

The Mānuš name, the *romeno lap,* is a unique sound combination, an indicative that dances in space and sets hearts into motion. A cause of joy that stops being heard when its bearer dies. This name, a unique combination among the sounds of the universe, is a marker of the uniqueness of each Mānuš individual in society, not because it announces his or her solitude but, on the contrary, because it announces his or her belonging to a close-knit group. In the preceding chapter I discussed the import of the different modes of presence of the dead and of the living. The deceased's siblings cease to utter his or her name. In contrast, the names of the living are constantly repeated: *"Oh Jé Garçounet! Garçounet, mur Garçounet, ap dox te pīje i dap mancax! Vo frō me Garçounet te pījes mancax!"* This practice and the sonorous richness of Mānuš names stand out against the usual laconism of individuals and gives to interactions between the living a force, a liveliness, a color, and a feel for life that conversation in no other society in the world can match.

romeno lap	**name for the Gadzos**
nickname, family name, abbreviation of given name, regular noun, onomatopoeia	given name + family name
used in the Mānuš community	used when interacting with Gadzos
unlimited stock, names are not transmissible	limited stock, names are transmissible
minimal repetition	much repetitiveness
name disappears with death	can be used again after death

We find here again the distinction between that which disappears, which characterizes the individual, and that which remains. The *romeno lap,* the actions and events of an individual's existence—these contrast with that which stands for the group: the "name for the Gadzos," the tomb . . . There can only be one Nīni, one Moreno, one Garçounet . . . while there will always be Alfred L.'s, Antoine L.'s, Baptiste L.'s . . . "There are always lots of L.'s," say the Gadzos. (I can add to this anecdote that it is interesting for another reason: it shows the ignorance of the Gadzos regarding the Mānuš, and that familiarity can accompany this ignorance: to the café owner, Garçounet is neither Garçounet nor Alfred L. but Fredo.)

SILENCE

The silence enveloping Mānuš totality, silence that is the Mānuš totality, constitutes a lack in the discourse of the Gadzos. Like all the things that establish and secure Mānuš integrity (the *mūlengre placi,* the places no longer frequented, the activities no longer practiced, the words and the names no longer uttered, the goods and dishes no longer consumed, the "happy idleness"[12]), this silence challenges Gadzo sovereignty over the universe. It is the Mānuš reclaiming of the self, of the world, but a reclaiming that makes it appear that Mānuš presence is no more a breach of Gadzo sovereignty than Gadzo omnipotence troubles the integrity of the Mānuš. Only analysis shows the establishment of Mānuš coherence

as a fracture, or an irregular series of fractures, in the Gadzo universe—
in the universe.

For the Gadzos, this seems like nothing: the Mānuš are at best a presence that doesn't mean anything to them. They dwell in vacant spaces
that Gadzos furnish with their imaginings, their illusions, to the point of
claiming the Mānuš to be illusory and phantasmagoric (there is a discourse claiming that the "Gypsies" are a myth created by the West and
that the Mānuš, Rom, Sinti, etc. don't exist [Martinez 1979]).

Though Mānuš identity is constituted with the establishment of emptiness, with discontinuity, discreteness, uncertainty, and silence, and
though these are essential properties, this doesn't prevent this identity
from being experienced as plenitude. The modes of transmission of
practices and knowledge evidence this. There is no room for teaching
and apprenticeship. This seems logical, since what needs to be acquired
is not the knowledge of a corpus of dogma and rules, even though as we
have seen there are rules, those of "respect," but mostly the ability to
observe, analyze, and interpret. Everything, and thus not just matters
concerning the dead, is transmitted in the mode of the "already known."
The first time the members of the X family invited me to participate in
their libations at a cemetery, they told me in French, "you know, what we
do by the tombs, you know . . ." Luckily I didn't have to rely only on
them to know! Teaching occurs as if the matter to be transmitted were
not a reality made up of fullness and emptiness, but a compact whole to
which one can only adhere. The aim is the feeling of integrity and permanence. It's everything or nothing. One doesn't become a Mānuš gradually: "it's in the blood." The person making an error (who is not making
the gestures expected of him or her) or who hesitates (is asking questions that shouldn't be asked—or is simply asking questions) is treated
as *iālo*. *Iālo* is a qualitative applied mainly to the Gadzos. There is no one
more *iāle* than Gadzos, it's of their essence to be so. The meaning of the
word, "raw," speaks for itself.

And yet given the nature of the rituals and the modes of affirmation,
there is room for uncertainty. Everyone within the community is at all
times in the process of observing themselves and each other, of won-
dering whether this is really the right way to do things. I have already
mentioned the young man who refused to lend his father's *pétanque* balls

to his cousin because they had belonged to his "late father." His refusal was met with rancor. A few days later, he told me he had decided to throw his father's *pétanque* balls down a well; was that the right thing to do? In his uncertainty he had nonetheless chosen the right solution: that of the absence of traces, the absence of troubles, the state of silence, of integrity—of "respect." But such questioning is done in private, alone (or with someone like the ethnographer), there is no public debate. The questioning must remain a silent one because it breaches integrity: it leaves room for the possibility of error. But that possibility must be eliminated. As we have seen in terms of evoking the past, it is only done when the person doing it is certain not to make a mistake, of "not lying," *te xoxap gar ap leste.* In other words, the person making the evocation must be certain it will perfectly coincide with the past events and persons that are being evoked ("to step in the footsteps of the defunct so perfectly that the traces are in no way changed"—which is again in Mā-nuš discourse rendered in terms of "respect"). The exploration of the past is of no interest. What could knowledge of history bring if not the discovery of a process? The Mānuš have not always been what they are today. They might not even have been always Mānuš (Indians, or Europeans, vagabonds or peasants, servants or warriors . . . they could have been any of the hypotheses that have been formulated as to their origin). It is better not to know.

To say nothing about oneself, to control one's appetites, to destroy objects so that they don't' leave any traces, "to forget" the history of those who have died and to silence their names, not to enter into activities suggested or imposed by the Gadzos (or to do this only temporarily and on one's own terms), to avoid public functions to which one has been invited . . . These are all the same gesture. It's always a question of integrity. So that the living be assured of their immutability, of their existence, it is necessary for the dead to lie in peace. The "late father's" *pétanque* balls?—at the bottom of the well! The "late husband's" truck?—to the junkyard! "It's better this way," states the family. As if the least breach, the least opening offered to the Gadzos could be fatal.

I AM NOW READY TO PROPOSE AN ANSWER to the question "why?" In the preceding chapter, when discussing the homage paid to the dead, I described how meaning, Mānuš meaning that is, came to be constituted.

This chapter must now answer the following question: Why, in order to insure their advent, did the Mānuš privilege the means of homage to the dead?

In order to constitute their presence, they have chosen to refer to real absence. They chose loss to insure their advent within the Gadzo world, that is, within fullness. They chose that which no longer exists so that they may exist as if they weren't here. The gestures establishing the integrity of the group are constructed around an irreparable wound inflicted upon that very integrity. Is it really irreparable? Yes, if we consider the individual. No, if we consider the member of the group who, being dead, becomes its founder and warrantor. The irreparable becomes the permanent—and we have seen that homage rituals make sensible the dimension of the irreparable at the same time as that of permanence. The finality of death is all the more attached to the advent of the Mānuš in that it is tied to individual death. The ungraspable nature of meaning, the invisible part of inscription, partakes of the advent. We can then understand that inscription is at the same time emancipation. Silence becomes the guarantor of the incorruptibility of identity, of the immutability of the group.

FOUR

The Basket Makers Have Become Scrap-Iron Dealers

In the olden days, said an elderly lady, we were always hiding in the
bushes. We didn't have a good life. Now, we can see that we have been
tamed like everyone else and words come easy to us, like everyone else . . .
An "old lady" at the official campsite La Jaunaie, set up
for the "Gens du Voyage" at Laval (Daniel Bizeul 1987)

THE WAY THE WORLD IS GOING

They lived in horse-drawn wagons and camped on riverbanks. They
could have been the models for the Gypsies of children's books. Did
those passing by in automobiles on nearby roads notice them? They had
the art of finding paths leading nowhere to shelter them. Sometimes
smoke rising behind a clump of trees would attract the eye. Or again, at
one end of a bridge, several brightly painted wagons would splash suddenly onto the landscape as if tossed haphazardly upon the shore of the
Allier. Did they do this to park and observe? The men seated on the
grass were weaving osier, the women wandered from one fire to another,
children stopped in their tracks and pointed at the stranger, dogs barked
. . . How to become part of this scene? When I began to follow Moršela
during summer vacations on expeditions lasting several days with the
Mānuš of the old wagons, I discovered the journeys that had to be taken
along paths at dawn to bring back the horses from the fields where, during the night and unbeknownst to the farmers, they had been put out to
pasture. We then had to rekindle the fire for morning coffee, and the
smell of wet wood permeated our clothes. When the sun was up, we cut
wild osier on the islands that emerge in summertime when the river
flows at its lowest. My head was heavy by then from lack of sleep, dizzy
from the smell of thistles, and I was almost moved to tears (hunger had
set in since breakfast) upon seeing the women come back from their day

of peddling. They were bringing back eggs, ham hocks, and chicken, and they carried loafs of bread under their arms, leaving traces of flour on their black skirts . . . It could happen that a convoy of wagons would cross a village. The men on foot would lead the horses hitched to the trailers as the women stopped and knocked at the doors of the low houses, the children spreading out all over the streets while the youngest ones remained on the eiderdown on the bed in the back of the wagons, standing up to peek through the little windows, two or three colts tied by a rope to the end of the wagons trailing behind.

Did the peasants of the Combrailles and the Limagne regions share my fascination? Or were they seeing only the torn and dirty clothes, the dilapidated state of some of the wagons, with their flaking paint of clashing colors, sheets of metal poorly attached to the roof to cover spots where the shell had rusted, and the panes missing from some of the windows and the hinges from the front doors? Women kept on begging and the men did not know how to talk inside the stores; they were yelling as if they were outdoors, as if (and this was indeed the case) they had never lived in a house. There were disabled people among them, individuals missing a limb, limping, or feeble minded, and they were not kept hidden. Peasants and Mānuš shared the same lack of concern for their bodies. On feast days, the lace blouses or the ribbons in the hair that both Gypsy and peasant women would wear appeared extraneous. At that time, at the end of the sixties, the rumor spread among these Mānuš families that the prefect of the *département* of Puy-de-Dôme had enacted a regulation that would force those *SDF* [the homeless] whose wagons were in too dilapidated a shape to replace them. Anxious couples were joking about the time they would be forced to abandon *i phūro vāgo,* "the old car," and go back to wandering on the roads like they did as newlyweds.[1] I searched the archives but could never find any trace of this regulation. There was at Bord-l'Étang a cart builder who knew how to make beautiful and solid wagons for Mānuš families. Mānuš sometimes built more rudimentary ones themselves.

They did not all possess a wagon in the sixties. Tradition had it that it would be shameful for newlyweds to sleep in the home of one of their parents. They made their bed in the grass, on a tarp or a sheet of plastic, or on straw. In case of rain, they took refuge under a wagon. But there were also couples with children in this situation, as well as families that had burnt their wagon upon the death of the father, and sometimes elderly people whose children had married. In the same way as the Mānuš who first arrived in the area, these people wandered the roads with baby buggies in which they piled up their belongings. And, as in Nēlo's story (note 1), they wandered along the roads followed by their dogs. In summer they too slept in the open; in winter they sought out the shelter of a barn or a bridge, or, if they were able to stay some time in the same spot, they built themselves makeshift shelters.

So were they masters of the woods and fields or just destitute? But why must their truth lie in one of these two images? What is at issue is not a distinction between the outside—the spectacle of these bits and pieces of misery—and the inside—the fullness of sensations they reserved for themselves (and immediately shared with someone who became close to them). Mānuš are like the *cajxi,* something that is not what it appears to be.

Does it matter whether people dwell only on those attitudes visible to outsiders or unveil those only the group members know? Likewise, the person who is mumbling as the fire next to which he is squatting throws sparks into the night, the person who is carefully disentangling a bunch of worn leather bridles, the person who gets drunk alone in the only café of a little hamlet and spills wine on the floor (it looks like he is doing it on purpose), they are busy with something else. They are busy with themselves. "Busy with themselves" means busy with their dead.

The Abbé Joseph Valet (1972b, 4) tells the following anecdote: One day he was looking for certain Mānuš families which he knew were camping at Gannat. He went there but did not find any of their wagons. He then asked an inhabitant of the burg if he knew where Monsieur X and Monsieur Y had gone. The villager answered, "You call that 'Monsieur,' I call that a bohemian."[2] Anthropology has for some time taught us not to be surprised at the gap between the complexity of the symbolic apparatus human beings invent and the material sparsity of their existence; between the impression of confusion that anthropologists sometimes get from frequenting them and the mastery over the universe they find when accomplishing their rituals. And history teaches that always within a human group's "civilization" or "culture" there is something that transcends its members. With the Mānuš we are beyond the distinctions between the sacred and the everyday, the prestigious and the ordinary. The presence of the dead sticks to every gesture. Thus why should they care to conform to the image others have of them? The speed with which they have abandoned everything that in their life carried a romantic image (wagons, horses, treks on the small roads away from highways . . .) shows this well. Does this mean that they were not sensitive to the charms of that lifestyle? Eršto stops his trailer among others in a parking lot near a church. He notices a small grassy knoll above some gardens. His truck barely unhitched, he grabs a bottle of wine and a glass and gets me to go there with him. As soon as his butt hits the grass he sighs: "*Kate, um bon* . . ." During a funeral I see Frantz again. I remember his big green trailer, decorated with a frieze of varnished wood made up of clumps of carved intertwined leaves. Now he has shown up with a Citroën "tube"[3] he has set up to sleep in. He invites me in: on the bare wall of the truck is a mirror framed by a horse collar decorated with a multitude of small copper bells, and thus the presence of another universe appears . . . And the Mānuš have all have kept the passion for wandering in the fields and for the animals they hunt, care for, train . . . The first clue that Vejs is no longer in deep mourning is that she buys a dozen hens she lets run around her trailer.

And yet some things were more important than a close connection with the horses and the pleasure of long walks on summer mornings. When, in a family, a brother turned in the horse and wagon for a car or a truck and a trailer, there was no longer the need to hitch up the whole convoy to ply one's trade in a village that might be twenty kilometers away or to greet cousins said to be somewhere else in the area. They no longer needed to be concerned with pastures near the campsite and, at any rate, they preferred to stop on a paved lot, because with the first rains, the going and coming of vehicles would quickly turn the grass into mud. At first, they continued to frequent "small places," but the people who liked to stop only for the briefest of times and those who liked to stay for hours or days no longer disposed of the same amount of time and no longer used this time for the same things. How then could they remain brothers and sisters? In their rush to rekindle the harmony of a lifestyle in which they all moved at the same rhythm, men, still young, in their forties and thirties, sold their horse and bought a truck without having learned to drive (an old used "tube" cost less than a stallion), others turned in their wagon for a trailer without having the means to buy a vehicle to pull it. So they had a son, or a son-in-law, or a younger brother pull them. Twenty, thirty years later, those among this group who are still alive haven't changed: they still have themselves pulled.

Why did the people who chose to change lead the others and not the other way around? Because that's the way it always is, we can't escape the movement of the world. And then there's the desire to remain together, there's the need for unanimity so as to escape the impression that everything is changing, that we are changing. These wrinkles [*décalages*] and these "discontinuities" the Mānuš so elaborately introduce into the midst of the Gadzos, they don't want them among themselves.

Between 1962 and 1990, the population of the *département* of Creuse went down from 163,630 inhabitants to 131,367.[4] There was some population growth in Puy-de-Dôme (508,672 inhabitants in 1962 to 598,672 in 1990), but over the years this growth slowed down,[5] especially as the ratio of youths to old people diminished.[6] The exodus of the population was large and steady from 1954 to 1975. These were population movements to outside of the area but also from the countryside to industrial urban centers within the region itself, in this case mainly Clermont-Ferrand. Then the movement out of the region slowed down while the trend of people moving from rural areas to small urban centers, including Issoire, Riom, and others, continued (Goubet and Roucolle 1984). Did the "people of the bush" simply follow the trend of the region a bit late? The person who could be seen plaiting osier in the grass is today [1990] breaking down scrap metal in the dust. Around him there's a pile of used tires, a mound of automobile carcasses in pieces, dismantled gas stoves and washing machines, oil stains on the bare ground, trailers and pickup trucks bereft of wheels or with flat tires. All this points to a stay that, if not permanent, is of long duration and even includes the pretty touch of geranium window boxes on one or two trailers. There might be a fire, but we don't know if it's the convivial fire of yesterday around which men and women used to gather to while away the time or if it's one used to burn the rubber or plastic casing around metal wires in the process of being recycled. The basket makers have become scrap-metal dealers. And just as the basket makers did, they show the same aptitude in their guise of scrap-metal dealers of embodying the old stereotyped, romanticized images of the Gypsy.

At present we encounter most of the Mānuš families on lots at the margins of small towns: In Puy-de-Dôme there is Riom, Issoire, Billom, Vic-le-Comte, Maringues, Thiers, etc., while in Creuse there is Guéret, Aubusson, and La Souterraine. These lots belong to them outright or de facto from having occupied them for a number years. Does this mean that there is no longer any travel? It is probable that a "sedentary" scrap-iron dealer today covers more territory than a "nomadic" basket maker of twenty years ago. But when the first goes home, it's always to the same place. Individual travel solely motivated by economic factors and with just the car or the truck has supplanted family moves. Seasonal agricultural work and religious events (Catholic pilgrimages or Pentecostal conventions) have become the only occasions to hitch the trailer and to cover long distances, but this for trips of less than a month's duration. Whether for economic or familial motives, travel circuits have tended to become more and more regular: they include visits to close kin and prospecting in places where business has been conducted previously. The mixing of families that used to happen during the time of frequent travel, even on short distances, in "the time of the horses," has ceased. Only funerals still bring people together.

Today, when I arrive in the middle of the afternoon in one of those lots, regardless of the season of the year, I am sure to encounter idle men. They look up in the direction of the car without showing any surprise. These are the men of "the time of the horses." They are alone at that time of the day with the younger children. All the others are in school or gone to do the day's peddling and collecting. As they did in the "time of the horses," these men are squatting by a fire or sitting in the shade on the V hitch of a trailer. They invite me to share their wine, the same glass being used by everyone ("We all have the same illness, brother!"). When the schoolchildren return, they are sent out to buy more wine. And also, just as in the "time of the horses," there will not be much conversation while drinking.

For the Mānuš the "emptying of the countryside" has meant the end of a certain number of traditional economic opportunities along with the growing scarcity of the number of places where they can camp freely, as many open spaces and communal fields have been eliminated with the consolidation of agricultural properties. In urbanized areas, new zoning plans have often affected the places where nomads could previously camp freely. The collecting and selling of old metals has become the principal activity. The success of such an activity is linked to the regularity of collection and the storage possibilities. Sometimes the young men, when they go to check out a dump or to clear out scrap metal from a work site or a villa, bring along their mothers, wives, or sisters. The women continue their door-to-door selling to Gadzos, but with uneven success. They no longer trade baskets and lace for bacon and eggs, they sell sheets, blankets, tablecloths, and napkins . . . Some women, mostly widows, have gotten their driver's license. The complementarity between the men's crafts and the women's peddling no longer exists. Family allowances, the payment of which for all French families is contingent on the children's school attendance, have become an indispensable source of income. The advantage of being known in the social services, which Mānuš visit regularly, has helped lead people to what might appear as sedentarization. The end of the sixties was a time when a coherent policy pertaining to "nomadic persons or persons of nomadic origin" was established. In 1969, the anthropometric booklet that had been imposed in 1912 on the Mānuš along with all other groups French law referred to as "SDF, *sans domicile fixe*" ("without fixed domicile") was eliminated and new statuses proposed for *Forains* and *Nomades* ["itinerants" and "nomads"]. A host of measures pertaining to the "parking of the trailers," the "medical state of the family," the schooling of the children, etc. were enacted so as to bring about the assimilation of the *Gens du Voyage* ["Travel People"], an assimilation the authorities of the time believed to be linked to their sedentarization.

On certain lots there are some sheds made with planks or some prefab dwellings; these are usually rudimentary constructions that are used as community or gathering halls. Very seldom does a family make its home in one of these. There are on average five or six trailers per lot (usually about six persons per trailer, including adults and children, but there are also old couples living alone and extra-large families). There can be up to twenty trailers on a lot in winter. There are some nostalgic Mānuš who still travel a circuit between villages and hamlets year round, like Phrael and Zita with their "unmarried daughter" who drives their small truck. They both receive a small pension and no longer peddle. They draw one hundred francs from the post office[7] each time they arrive in a new canton.

A lot, dusty in summer, muddy in winter, is at once a place for living (people are sleeping in the trailers, children are running around at all times), a place of sociability (the men and women from the different households spend a lot of time conversing in the open spaces between the trailers), a place to raise animals (chicken, geese, and other fowl wander around), a place for storage (there are mounds of scrap metal, old tires, batteries, etc.) and for work (engines are repaired, bodywork is hammered out, and sometimes new basket seats are still plaited for old chairs, etc.). "The men from the time of the horses," the ones who had seemed to me to be the masters of the universe, masters of men and masters of nature, no longer have anything to do. They are not interested in cars, they don't touch scrap metal (often the younger men object when an older uncle or brother wants to work with iron: "it's not right to let them tire themselves that way"), and they don't enjoy walking in town.

At each new visit I am struck by the affection that unites kin from different generations. Toward children, the patience of these men from times past, those who between the silence and the yelling seem to know today only how to talk to and address each other as if they were still giving directions to their horses, is limitless: "yes my son," "yes my little girl" . . . I am quite sure that I have never heard them forbid something or refuse a request. At the worst of anger or drunkenness, when the insult they might be throwing at their wives or their brother becomes, it seems, charged with all the anger of the days of idleness, they also can open their arms to hug their grandson or granddaughter who might have chosen that very moment to seek shelter with them. The younger people, upon their return from the day's labors, unfailingly bring back to their elders a liter of wine, a six pack of beer, some cigarettes . . . Because he said he liked the cheerfulness brought to his trailer by a bullfinch he had captured during a walk with one of his grandsons, Yūdo now complains, even though he is touched by each gift, that his trailer has become overfilled with cages and the racket made by all the robins, parakeets, and other exotic birds whose names he doesn't know that his descendants now keep on giving him.

It can happen that lots bought for three or four households deteriorate with the growth in the number of families. Old trailers and trucks without wheels, which serve as shelters, multiply, while the piles of scrap metal and old tires get bigger. In Gadzos' eyes, it is as if the Mānuš had

The payment of a family allowance to families with children in France is contingent for all the population on the children's school attendance. But within the framework of the measures taken regarding the "nomads" beginning in 1969, they were required to carry a coupon booklet making it possible to instantly verify their children's absences. This coupon booklet had to be signed each month by a teacher or director of the school, though it is true that the number of allowed absences was somewhat higher for the children of the SDFs [*sans domicile fixe*, "without fixed domicile"] than for the rest of the population.

This system of control, over the course of the years and depending on the instructions of the various local institutions in charge of allocating the family allowance, has been applied with varying degrees of rigorousness. In the eyes of the administration, "our" scrap-metal dealers, whose driver's licenses label them all as "itinerant" or "nomad," are still categorized as SDF, or "homeless."

The Mānuš also had to carry in the past another booklet serving as ID. It had been required by a law passed in 1912 that required anyone without a fixed domicile and regular income to carry a "carnet de circulation," an anthropometric document that included photographs of the face and profile of the holder, his or her given names, family names, and nicknames, height, chest size, the bizygomatic width of the face, width and length of the head, the length of the right ear, the width of the middle and little fingers of the left hand, the width of the left elbow, and eye color. This law was aimed at the "bohémiens," the Gypsies, and was motivated by the two contradictory

given up their authenticity by giving up their wagons and horses. Now perceived as "deviance" or "weakness," their difference becomes something in need of correction. Their old activities, such as horse dealing and basket making, which entailed a certain degree of insertion into the local social fabric, have ended. Today, the Mānuš "arrive on the job market" without any training, and yet they do not become laborers. There are no salaried people among the members of the family I am writing about, though some spend short periods as woodcutters hired by the job at certain times in winter or do occasional seasonal agricultural work (picking apples and peas, participating in the grape harvest, etc.). From the small recycler to the wholesaler, the scrap-metal trade often works in a closed circuit among Travelers.

Gadzos perceive all recycling activities to be parasitic, and some also suspect the women's peddling at the doors of villas to be casing for future theft. They notice the presence of idle men all day long in the camp.

(*continued*)

purposes of controlling the Gypsies and getting rid of them by making their
lives impossible in France. The debates in the French senate preceding the
vote referred to "ethnic nomads." And in fact it was Gypsy groups that, before any other category of the population, were assigned these booklets.
Holders of these *carnets de circulation* were required to present them to the
police to be stamped upon their arrival and departure from a canton. The
members of the Mānuš families in this book have had to endure the regime
of the *carnet de circulation.* The Mānuš called it *u baro lil,* "the big booklet." A person was assigned one of these upon his or her fourteenth birth-
day. In addition to individual *carnets de circulation,* all heads of families
were also assigned a family booklet containing information about all the
members of the family and including health information. All the Mānuš of
the bushes grew old along with the *baro lil.*

The law of 1912 was only abrogated in 1969, when a new law was passed
assigning a new status to the nomads but still regulating their traveling practice, as it laid out rules applicable to persons "circulating in France without
any fixed domicile." This new law established four types of circulation practices, that is, four types of "carnet de circulation," classified on the basis of
type of domicile, fixed or nonfixed, and the degree of regularity of the income of the subject. Each category—each booklet type—was subjected to
varying constraints that have gradually become looser over the course of
the years, though they have yet to be completely eliminated. For instance,
the required visa went from monthly to trimonthly and eventually to yearly.

For many Mānuš, contacts with non-Gypsies are more and more limited
to the customers solicited during their circuits and to specialized func-
tionaries (social workers, gendarmes, teachers . . .) which society sends
to them. Mānuš and Gadzos share the impression that their relationship
has deteriorated.[8] The sense of solidarity between kin living on the same
lot became more intense while that between kin living in communities
more distant from each other lessened. On the other hand, these new
conditions led to closer acquaintance with neighbors whom the Gadzos also look upon as "bohemians" and "Gypsies" and who, at the close
of trajectories that have been at times identical and at times different,
ended up experiencing pretty much the same fate as "our" Mānuš.
These include the Yéniches, who, like the Mānuš, have abandoned bas-
ketry work and horse-drawn wagons, as well as the carnies who used to
have small booths at fairs held in "small places" and who had to become
junk and scrap-metal dealers with the decline in celebrations of local

patron saints in the region. Instead of a solidarity based on common values and knowledge, a new solidarity is woven between these groups, one based on the common social niche they have come to occupy. Sharing a common lifestyle and practicing the same activities play a role in the establishment of these relationships. Thus Mānuš frequent Pirde scrap-metal dealers ("they are Gadzos who now live like Travelers") while they shun the much more financially well-off Sinti carnival merchants (even though Sinti are, according to scholarly classifications, Tziganes belonging to the same category as Mānuš do). These contacts bring along cultural changes. For instance French, or more specifically the Traveler's argot,[9] is the language of these interactions.

In all the lots I visit, I get the same impressions, whether it be in the dull hours of the afternoon, the joyful ones of the morning when the young men wash themselves outside and get ready to go on their rounds, or those peaceful ones when, before the evening meal eaten early at the end of the afternoon, people from different trailers or fires talk to one another, invite each other for a drink, and linger to discuss the day's news one more time. Thus, in spite of the scattering of the Mānuš and the retrenchment of smaller groupings unto themselves, there is still the same uniformity that was so striking when Moršela and I used to travel from one wagon camp to another. The faces in the various encampments were different of course, but the feeling was that we were back in the same camp we had just left, as if it had been transplanted in a different place, albeit one not that different, as it was always "behind the bushes," always "at the end of a path," and always holding the same liveliness and joyful welcome. Mānuš still seem to live the same life everywhere. Conversations are the same, so are the jokes and the tones of voice, as well as the way the inside of the trailers are decorated and the style that, through a certain length of their skirts and a particular way of walking, young Mānuš women imprint on Gadzo fashion.

If Mānuš families everywhere have experienced the same evolution, is it because the Gadzo world doesn't leave them any choice? How can we claim that the Mānuš are not affected by the forces ruling the Gadzo world? And yet, how can we believe that the Mānuš are the Gadzos' playthings? Is it the evolution of the Gadzo world which dictates the form of the pompons decorating the curtains protecting the sleeping alcove at the back of the trailers? Does it make the Mānuš prefer to drink their wine in small cups of china or earthenware rather than glasses when a good bottle is opened, or that leads a person to give a sharp pinch on the nape a cousin's neck as a sign of affection after having teased him in front of everybody? Have the Mānuš not been instrumental in maintaining their own unanimity and integrity?

It is true that they do not need to consult each other, that they share an unspoken understanding, when an unpredictable event (quarrel, accident, death, . . .) brings them face to face; but do they seek this purposely? There is no explicit proclamation nor expressed will to resistance. But the young people are full of vigor, many among them have renounced alcohol, they have no intention of giving up being Mānuš; they want to remain true to their identity. Today as yesterday, they want to be in the gaps [*décalages*] they create in the world as it is. And they do not explain that the foundation for their certitude lies in the acts of homage they perform, in the feeling of loyalty to the generations that preceded them. They continue to refrain from uttering the names of their departed loved ones, they still stop at all the cemeteries where they have relatives buried, they still pour rum on the graves and converse with the dead.[10] They still deprive themselves of a dish or an entertainment while keeping silent about the reason for it; they still keep the truck that had belonged to a departed in the midst of other vehicles, this without putting a distinctive sign on it; they still hide the departed's rings in the back of drawers, tied into a handkerchief; they still carefully watch over the distribution and circulation of photographs on which the living and the dead mingle—and they don't talk about all this. It is important for them to maintain, not so much the content of these "ritual" gestures, but the possibility of incorporating them into all the circumstances of daily life.

It is tempting to link this ritual homage to the state of the world in which it takes place, that is, to link the establishment of the *mūlengre placi,* the picking of a horse which becomes *mullo,* the renouncing of hunting hedgehogs at night . . . , with the fencing of fields with hedges, the isolation of the farms where in the summer the women lead the cows back to the stable every evening, the bakers' practice of touring hamlets with a grocery van . . . Not much thinking is required to understand that this link would be illusory, as there is no relation of necessity between the attitude of the Mānuš toward their dead and peasant practices as they could be observed in the Auvergne and Limousin regions in the mid-sixties, except for what I noted earlier between the establishment of discontinuities and the filled-up, saturated character of the world as it is conceived by the Gadzos.

This possible illusion is accentuated by my own experience. I still remember the wagons parked by poplar groves, wine around summer campfires, afternoons lying on the grass while baskets seemed almost to make themselves, and then, as some of my companions passed away, I came to learn the gestures of exchange with the dead intertwined with all those events. Today when turning back to this past, I have the feeling of a concordance between the life of the Mānuš at the moment when I was allowed to enter it beyond what the outside world was allowed to see and the ritual apparatus through with they establish their presence in the world. Yet the younger Mānuš generations don't agree with my analysis. They know that it is the viewpoint of a Gadzo confusing reality with the images he has in his head. There is a dimension of Mānuš reality that changes, that which can be seen, and a dimension that is unchanging, that which cannot be seen. Having become scrap-metal dealers and illustrating all too well the weight of the sweat, labor, and dirt that comes with the generally held image of this activity, the Mānuš remain nonetheless capable of performing the gestures that put them in something like a state of grace, that puts them outside the world.

Mānuš are aware that it is of no import that they be basket makers or scrap-metal dealers, or that they conform to the Gadzos' view of them.

It would be absurd to claim that during the quarter of a century spanning 1965 to 1990 the Mānuš were not aware their lives were changing and were not affected by this change. There was no way of ignoring that the horses were disappearing, that the landscapes around the campsites were transforming, that new activities and habits had to be adopted and that the roles of each family member were not the same, that time was not spent the same way and that new faces were encountered. The following is a temporal marker: we used to drive from Gouzon to Riom on the *département* highway and stop to drink gray wine in bars at Mainsat, Pontaumur, Ours (but not in Pontgibaud, where we had had some trouble with the local gendarmerie). Now when I go to Montluçon I drive

nonstop at full speed on the tollway. It was thus during a period of transformation that I've had the privilege of establishing relationships with
certain families and that I was able, by following their life over the course
of the years, to uncover that which establishes Mānuš permanence in the
world.

A question arises: are the rituals of homage to the dead I am describing and the importance I see in them linked to this context of transformation? Should loyalty to the dead be interpreted as the group's will and
ability to remain a group? It could be that there has been a process of em-
phasizing these rituals, a process linked to the upheavals the Mānuš have
had to face. Very concretely, there were a great number of deaths, a generation of men decimated by alcohol . . . Could I have been under the illusion that I was giving an account of permanence while I was in fact
glossing over a crisis? The years I have been using as a reference for the
picture I have been evoking are filled with clamor and fury. I don't even
have to look through my field notes or my personal journal but simply
through notes in my date books from the time of Moršela's death (on
March 31, 1983 — but Moršela's death is a point of reference only for myself). Counting only those who were like brothers to me I find:

May 11, 1983: "and today it's Moreno who died."

March 14, 1984: "and now Garçounet."

September 24, 1985: "Gogo in the hospital, no hope."

January 12, 1986: "Hospital of Riom."

January 28, 1986: "Riom, Notre-Dame de Marturé, 4:30 P.M."

August 18, 1986: "*Lebo, čele menši vianle.*"

November 18, 1987: "Hospital Montluçon (tel. 70-02-30-30): *Mur
Dēvel!* C'est pas vrai qu'il avait cet âge-là!" ["It can't be that he was
only that old!"]

November 22, 1987: "Hāzo: bad illness."

April 3, 1988: "and now Tīni is in the hospital."

April 5, 1988: "When we depart, Yūdo and I embrace — is it for the
last time? (It's always the same with them: I want to make grand
declarations, I say them in my head, and then when with them I say
almost nothing. And then after I leave I think again and realize that

the grand declarations were communicated. Without having to say anything)."

July 1, 1988: "Yūlo. There was no message."

August 2, 1988: "death of Pulfe's baby."

December 28, 1989: "*ǯā pal u kuč Milo. Ap u grābli:* someone and something did exist: they no longer exist."

January 28, 1991: "Jo's death: *jop nina:* **la boisson** . . .*"

And I am not even counting the funerals[11] . . . Perhaps laying down the dead amongst them, perhaps this is a way of accepting, and thus of erasing, the misfortune pursuing them.

YEARS OF CLAMOR AND FURY? What clamor?

The clamor of evenings of wine drinking? Several times Djīvi, in the throes of one of the crises of alcohol intoxication that gripped him in the middle of the night, set fire to his trailer. (After the marriage of his only son, he found himself alone with his wife. As he did not have a driver's license, his sons-in-law took turns pulling his trailer. He changed trailers often and yet his always looked battered, mistreated. Djīvi would attack it with punches and kicks when rage would sweep over him, "without reason," bemoaned his wife. She was the petite Papi, who at such times would curl up against the wheel of a truck and cry.)

Or again, could it be the clamor of proclamation of allegiance to the "Lord"? The conversion to Pentecostalism that began in the course of those years possibly bears witness to the reality of a crisis. Pentecostalism is a religious movement of messianic inspiration that started in the United States at the beginning of the twentieth century and is part of Christian Protestantism. The first Gypsy conversions occurred in France in 1952, in the western part of the country, among Mānuš families close to those of the Central Massif. These families were frequenting rural zones, searching bushes, and living in horse-drawn wagons (Le Cossec 1991). In 1957, Pastor Le Cossec, member of the Assemblies of God and a Breton Gadzo who had baptized the first converted Mānuš, decided to form the Gypsy Evangelical Mission and train preachers among the Gypsies themselves. From that moment on, the movement grew rapidly, spreading to all Gypsy groups, in France and outside of France.[12]

In France, the journal *Le XXe siècle fédéraliste,* published by the Protestant Federation of France, gave figures of 30,000 "baptized" in June of 1985, 60,000 "faithful" more or less regularly attending events organized by the Gypsy Evangelical Mission, and 450 Gypsy ministers. These figures seem credible to me. The movement kept on growing, even though less rapidly than in the sixties and seventies. Social scientists link the growth of these sorts of religious phenomena to contexts of crisis or transition, particularly when they occur amidst oppressed populations, as for instance in situations of colonization, exploitation, exclusion, or uprooting (Lanternari 1983). Jean-Pierre Liégeois (1983, 141) argues that Gypsy Pentecostalism can be seen as both a "sign of a social disorganization" and "a protest in the process of structuration, one transcending social divisions." Alain Bourdin sees it as a reaction to urbanization:

> With long-term stay on a lot, the modes of social regulation and rejuvenation that were accomplished through dispersal and regrouping disappear. There is a risk that the cycles of high interaction followed by periods of calm could be replaced by a sort of flattening of everyday life . . . Thus there is ground for wondering whether Pentecostalism, which reintroduces excitement to social life and turns the excluded into the elect might constitute . . . a form of response to assimilation. (Bourdin 1984, 28)

Jean Baubérot (1988, 122) also evokes "the Gypsies' main problem," that is, "the extension in these past few decades of the main characteristics of modern urban society to the whole of the French space." Richard Glize (1989, 441–42) sees a "possible new cultural engagement," in which Pentecostalism would be offering "a great common reference" that Gypsy groups would need in order to "oppose and stake their ground in the face of non-Gypsy society and power."

Pentecostalism announces the return of Christ on earth in the near future, but, in contrast to other messianic movements, it doesn't set a date. In order to be saved during the day of reckoning, the converted henceforth live their lives according to the "word of God" as it is revealed essentially in the New Testament. Pentecostalism involves as well core references to the Holy Ghost to which are linked some of the deepest experiences a member can live through: speaking in tongues[13] and miraculous healing.[14]

The faithful regularly gather in assemblies (in permanent structures or in itinerant tents). These meetings involve singing, testimonials by the converted, reading and commenting on the Bible, and prayer. Moments of great cordiality and familiarity (we are brothers and sisters) and moments of great intensity (when God is addressed) alternate. There is a mass every Sunday, when the faithful partake of the bread and the wine. Every year, the Gypsy Evangelical Mission organizes large gatherings called Conventions attended by members from several countries.

Thus the converts speak publicly and individually to announce that they are reborn. They are no longer the same parents or spouses in their individual lives, now guided by the "word of truth," and they reject the world's temptations (Williams 1989). In their collective life they now belong to the "Christian people," to those who, like themselves, have answered the Lord's call. In order to merge the notions of "Christian people" and "Gypsy people," preachers point out the coincidence they see between "biblical laws" and the traditions of Gypsy communities.[15] In this, Pentecostal Gypsy discourse makes a claim on the transformation of Mānuš converts in their universal dimension (that is, they are now new men and women) as well as on the permanence of their specific dimension (they remain Mānuš—but they are better than Mānuš in that they are now conscious of the concordance of Mānuš ways of life with divine commandments).[16] Moreover, this "Gypsy people," making its appearance with the conversion, includes individuals and groups that in the past had called themselves Sinti, Mānuš, Gitanos, Rom, Roma, Voyageurs, Yéniches, etc. etc. There can be incompatibilities at times between the traditional affirmation of community ("we Rom," "we Mānuš" . . .) and the new claim to totality ("we Christians"), which leads to objections for instance to certain economic practices such as fortune-telling and theft and certain ritual practices such as offerings to the dead. The Pentecostal ideal calls for matching traditional customs with biblical commandments: anything that doesn't lend itself to this is then denounced as a superstition and must disappear.

The first conversions among the Mānuš of Puy-de-Dôme and Creuse occurred at the end of the sixties, precisely during those years when the transition from basket making to scrap-metal dealing was beginning to make its mark. I am not able to tell the proportion of converted families. They amount possibly to half the people, perhaps a bit more. The reason for the difficulty of coming up with precise figures lies in the special nature of Pentecostal conversion among "our" Mānuš' in contrast to other Pentecostal Gypsies and even other Pentecostal Mānuš. It is, again, something they don't talk about. It would thus be very difficult to research this matter. We encounter among them a few pastors and preachers, and they, like all spokespersons for the movement, are tireless proselytizers. But the others, the "ordinary followers," don't say anything. Even during the months following their baptism they don't behave at all like other new converts, who usually are always explaining their choice, showing off and spreading their new beliefs and proclaiming their transformation. In the absence of this, how do we know they are Pentecostal? In the towns where their lots are located or in neighboring towns, they attend meetings that bring together converted Voyageurs, Yéniches, and Mānuš, but they are rarely seen on the stage when it comes time to testify. At times they hitch their trailers to attend a Convention. In their homes among the photographs of the deceased there might appear a cross beneath the inscription "Jesus is our Lord," and a bible might be carefully placed on a lace doily by the bedstead. They no longer have their children baptized at the local parish church or send for priests for the funerals of their loved ones, but if one of their Catholic relatives dies they do attend the Catholic services. In conversations the French expression "Le Seigneur!" ["The Lord!"] competes with the older Mānuš "Oh Jeses!" or "Mur Dēvel!" They frequently exchange audiotapes with songs and religious testimonies, and young men can be seen repairing automobile engines to the sound of canticles from the car radio.

The question that arises is whether Pentecostalism partakes of the relation Mānuš–Gadzo, the dimension that I have described as visible and changing, or of the relation Mānuš–Mānuš, the one I have described as invisible and unchanging. Does Pentecostalism lie on the side of noise or on that of silence? Experts' analyses and preachers' harangues invite it to be placed into the movement of the world. As for myself, I am sometimes tempted to argue that Pentecostalism might have replaced the bushes. Sheltered behind the concrete wall that is the profession of faith, Mānuš can keep on being Mānuš (something that is beyond the Pentecostal engagement just as it is beyond such activities as basket making or scrap-metal dealing . . .). They can thus, without anything disturbing them, keep on being Mānuš among themselves.[17] But Pentecos-

talism aims to intervene in the dimension of silence and thus includes
homage to the dead among the "superstitions" it denounces.[18]

Is this aim credible? Once, on the first day of the year, when we were
coming back from the cemetery, where we had gone to put some flowers on graves and had drunk a bottle of rum and talked to the departed,
I remarked to my companions, who were all "baptized," that they were
no longer supposed to perform these gestures. Their reaction was unequivocal; they said something like the following: "Oh really! The day
we won't do these things, now that would be the end of everything!" In
their eyes, their Pentecostal faith is in no way competing or in opposition with loyalty to their dead. There is no interference, because the two
domains are not connected. The only possible way of depicting their relationship would be as one of juxtaposition.[19]

I am less troubled by the noisy attacks on traditional homage during
Pentecostal ceremonies than by the silence of the Mānuš regarding their
conversion, the silence of the Mānuš of the bushes, of the Mānuš of the
lots where scrap metal is now recycled. I know them only too well to ignore that, for them, the things that are not talked about are the important
ones. Homage to the dead also partakes of the "worldly" dimension of
existence, as it must be remembered that it is often in function of the respect they show toward their dead that relationships are established between Mānuš or between Mānuš and other communities "of the travel."
Pentecostalism modulates these relationships according to a new regime. This involves a number of experiences, some properly religious,
such as the emotion of collective prayers and the joyfulness of the songs,
and some linked to daily life, including the fatigue and the trials met in
the course of travel to the gatherings, the Gadzo hostility that has to be
dealt with, and the moments of relaxation between ceremonies. These
experiences are shared by converts belonging to different communities.
Common memories are built. If it happens that in the public definition
of identity, the reference to Pentecostal values supplants reverence for
the dead, does this not point to the possibility that the relation Mānuš–
Mānuš is no longer constructed in the dimension of silence but in that
of noise? In that case, relations with the dead would lose their central
place, that crucial place from which they accompany in silence all the
gestures of daily life. Once the external rationale for performing these
gestures—that is, to distinguish oneself from others—finds a system that

performs better or that is better adapted to the new social context, then the internal rationale of "it's in the blood" would no longer suffice to insure the maintenance of this set of attitudes. Only "survivals" would be left, ineffective, rootless gestures. The feeling of a necessity that cannot be questioned would be lost. There would remain only a loyalty without any stakes, a tenderness: we are doing this because of our elders, because they were doing it . . . And then the signs would be abandoned, and, one day, a new generation would wake up with the idea that it's no longer worth it.[20] The world would keep on going, but it would have lost some of its substance. Mānuš silence would no longer speak. The Mānuš would let the truth about them and about the time of their reign be lost. Perhaps no one would believe that such Mānuš ever did exist. And yet the Mānuš would not have disappeared: they would have invented new ways of being Mānuš in the midst of the Gadzos. But how could we believe that the end of the Mānuš who had chosen to install themselves in the world through silence would not take something away from the world?

When trying to answer these questions, we are of course (and I am tempted to say "luckily") stymied by the silence of the Mānuš, by the kind of certitude that silence always gives them an answer to everything. And what if, more so than loyalty to the dead, what we have seen is actually a loyalty to silence?

SILENCE

Choosing silence means that the essential and the public are not communicating. The essential is incorruptible, unassailable, it cannot be encroached.

Silence, from a Mānuš perspective: I do not disturb anything, I do not signal, but also there is nothing that can disturb me, I am not vulnerable.

The Gadzos, that is, everyone around me discoursing and busying themselves, cannot affect my quality of being Mānuš, the circle of silence I have dug at the center of the world.

I am attached to the dead—which constitutes me—through certain particular gestures that I am performing. But these gestures are mixed up with and so similar to all the gestures of everyday life, the gestures made by the men and women I encounter every day in the streets of my town, the gestures made by all the people I never meet (I see them from the end of my lot speeding on the freeway, I imagine their lives when watching TV . . .), so that, except for my brother or sister, no one can know that in those gestures, in even a hint or a fragment of such a gesture, the most ordinary gesture that can be, there lies the totality of the world I have seized, the world that I possess, that possesses me.

Thus permeating all appearances, that which constitutes me frees daily life from the trivial and the transitory. All the gestures of life are so intimately a part of me that, whatever I might be doing, I am giving of myself completely, but invisibly—I give myself to being Mānuš.

The Mānuš are like the *cajxi* they sow along the roads.

UP TO NOW IN MY DESCRIPTION, I have considered the ordinary dimension of the gestures of homage to the dead as primary and their ritual dimension as secondary and, in some ways, as an addition to the everyday which it transforms. Let us for a moment attempt to invert this relationship and imagine that this inversion is the way the Mānuš see it. It then appears that ritual is no longer added to the everyday but that the everyday shelters ritual, that is, the properly Mānuš. But how can the "properly Mānuš" be perceived if it thus permeates all appearances? There's nothing to distinguish the marked sign (I no longer drink wine as homage to my dead brother) from the trivial gesture (I no longer drink wine because I have an ulcer). There is no clear ritual way or voice. There is an individual decision (but I don't announce it) and a selection (I pick only certain gestures, and who could know?). Thus all the random gestures of everyday life appear as so many miscues aimed at those who would map the Mānuš way, identify it, isolate it. And how is it that the Mānuš themselves don't get lost in such a forest? The perception of meaning for them is first of all a question: *cajxi.*

If the Mānuš voice doesn't make a sound, how is it that the Mānuš can hear it? It's in their head. The Mānuš do hear the Mānuš voice in their heads. They hear it as they hear everything pertaining to the dead. When they are together, without the need to explain anything but simply by seeing the way others are acting, they know they all have the same voice in their heads. It is necessary for the Mānuš to come together, to spend time together. The Mānuš voice, silence, links the Mānuš to each other. No Mānuš wants to deviate, yet they all also know that alone they cannot invent this way; they must rely on the others as much as on themselves to be able to vouchsafe the correctness of their actions. A Mānuš could say: If I am the only one to perform these gestures, even if I am performing them perfectly, they are meaningless. That which constitutes me only belongs to me if I share it. I have total trust in my fellow Mānuš (without questioning them, without asking something of them), and I know that this trust will not be betrayed. They are my brothers and my sisters.

This then explains the statement I made at the beginning of this book, that when it comes to the Mānuš, one can only be completely in or irremediably out. With each return, everything seems untouched, intact. And then if one gets in, if one has on other occasions spent enough time to get in, there's the immediate feeling of finding again the deepest of complicity. The months of absence are of no import. There's no need to talk. This is indeed the crux: after several months, after several years, there's no need to talk. It's November; we are returning from wandering in the fields, three companions in a wagon that the women have left to us: this quietude of the waning day, and the wine in the liter bottles, the cigarettes burning between the fingers, no words uttered, warmth, love . . . and it lasts, the only event is that of the waning light.

There is thus no speech, no matter how elaborated or hermetic, that can be the equivalent of this silence, because, in the end, there's no discourse that can resist exegesis or being taken apart, that can survive the deployment of explanation. Only silence can speak the whole.

A Mānuš would say: Why should I enter through my intellect into something whose heart I inhabit? I feel no need to dominate this silence to which I belong. What is the use of these gestures that unite me at once with my dead and with my brothers and sisters (those who have the same dead as me, and those who are making the same gestures as me for their dead)? I don't know. *žāno gar.* The dead must not be used. Respect. *Ēra.*

The temptation to comment and to elucidate disappears in the face of the feeling of necessity. Certainly, this can be better transmitted when one doesn't know what it means. The understanding of things doesn't generate the necessity of doing them, as it reveals that we are the one doing these things and not the other way around. The day the feeling of belonging to silence comes to be succeeded by the certitude that I am the one inventing silence, that day would mark the advent of signs, those cultural signs apt to be exhibited, exalted, claimed . . . These signs that the Gadzos expect from the Mānuš. It would be the advent of noise.[21]

The Mānuš way/voice is at once acceptance (and taking possession) of the universal: it is all the gestures of life, of the world, of the everyday; and the affirmation of an irreducible singularity: it cannot be reproduced, translated, it is betrayal-proof, incorruptible—it cannot be led astray.

Could a consequence of these modes of constitution, of the tireless construction of that which cannot be said, be a state of daze? I remember Moršela filled with resolve, the resolve of a Hun warrior, after barely taking the time to wash up on the morrows of our night expeditions. He was getting a head start, *ap u grābli,* "to the graves," because nothing had happened during the night's journey (no incidents, no trouble), and we had to go thank the dead for this nothing . . . (This could have happened after the evening we had, on a whim, after ten P.M., decided to go visit Butcho or Nēgui more than a hundred kilometers away. We had to go wake up Pierrot Paillon, the gas pump owner, to fuel up and then stop at *mère* Amandine's, who luckily at this late hour was still playing cards with her customers, and buy a liter of wine for the road. Moršela, when going to the same place on another night, had heard women's screams even though he was driving full speed with all of his truck windows closed, so he didn't want to go by the village of Joze, and we made a detour that added twenty kilometers to the trip. When we had arrived at the encampment where three days earlier Nēgui had kept us for dinner, there were still a great many trailers, but Nēgui was no longer there, having left that morning for Billom to go to his brother-in-law "in a fit of anger." He had probably gotten into an argument, and now our arrival there in middle of the night woke everybody. Even people who were not part of our circle of well-known acquaintances got up and came to inquire of the reasons for our visit. We couldn't leave right away, we had to talk, listen, drink a glass of wine, a cup of coffee . . . Finally we got back on the road and arrived at Nēgui's, but he didn't seem particularly happy to see us: were we going to stay the night? Our initial excitement that had propelled us on the journey had died down, and at any rate Moršela explained to Nēgui that we hadn't just come to see him, we had business in Issoire, and we preferred to drive on the highway at night so we had just stopped to say hello . . . Back in the car we were getting tired, we made one more stop at the snack bar of the train station in Clermont, one of the few places, though not a very welcoming, that stayed open at that time of the night. Then we were back on the roads of the bush country, where we did not encounter any other car.)

Another world exists in this world, and this other world is the Mānuš domain: they have nothing to say about it. But once we inhabit "this other world" (once we are inhabited by it), this world beneath, this world of silence, of invisibility, how can we come back to the world above, the world of manners, of appearance? Often, in the midst of the Gadzos, the Mānuš give the impression that they are locked into their world, as would someone not able to recover from a too violent revelation. Is not this distance [décalage] the one "the men from the time of the horses" are trying to maintain at the moment when the movement of the world has destroyed their lives? And what of all this alcohol they're drinking? Alcohol has to do with stupor, with daze, with the feeling of detachment, of dissociation, toward the universe—could it be that it is being used to insert one of those "gaps" through which the Mānuš establish themselves?

But could this daze be my own reaction rather than that of the Mānuš? The reaction of one who is intent on linking up bits and pieces collected in the course of the years so as to reconstitute a coherence and then stop and contemplate it, rather than the reaction of those who are ceaselessly constructing the invisible through all of their gestures? But then why, to Yūdo, to Mideli, to Štako, to Moršela and others, would things not reveal themselves as a whole? We were walking among the fires which were now dying down in the deserted encampment, the women having gone on their day's circuit, or to cut osier, to wander the fields, or to see what was happening "in the country." Yūdo stood in front of the Puys mountain range on the horizon, and he explained that there, by taking a given fork in the road at the base of that mountain, and another road leading to the other side, and behind this wood that looked like a black spot, or below this hill covered with grape wines that could be seen on the left side . . . there were other camps, and there and there and there, there were graves, mūlengre placi, signs and traces . . . And thus truth is revealed and the universe tips over—the Mānuš' mastery over the world. And Yūdo in the midst of the trailers starts to sway, as if dazed. To someone who would have observed him from the road above, he might have appeared drunk, or dizzy, as someone suddenly lost in familiar surroundings.

I began this book with the description of the world beneath, that of
the dead among the living, which is also the revelation waiting at the end
of my reconstruction. I did this because I am trying to convey the feeling that everything is given instantaneously all at once. I am trying to
provoke a daze, to immediately establish the real: to show rather than
explain. There is nothing to look for beyond this description; it is useless to dig. In the world above, yes, images do accumulate: basket makers, scrap-metal dealers, Pentecostals . . . It might be that the ritual dimension is exhausted in the dimension of the everyday so much that it
blends with it. So to describe minutely the attitudes and habits of the
Mānuš, we would, at the same time, have to succeed in bringing to light
the whole of the apparatus of silence that makes them the masters of the
world, or at least convey the feeling that beneath this reality, there exists
yet another, a denser, more vibrant one (the very same feeling torment-
ing the art lover in the story of the painting beneath the painting[22]).[23]
But by proceeding that way, we too might risk running endlessly behind
the real, behind Mānuš silence, and thus irremediably miss it. So I preferred to describe without delay that which cannot be said or seen.

COULD THE SILENCE OF THE COMMUNITY about itself be tempting individuals to be mute about themselves, to make them unconcerned about
letting outsiders know who they are? It is true that the Mānuš, and more
particularly these Mānuš, seem quite laconic. Modesty (*i lač,* "shame")
is one of their most important social values. It is unseemly to express
one's feelings. If someone wants to interrupt a conversation (and not
only a conversation between Mānuš and Gadzos), the most efficient way
is to start asking questions. The Mānuš will not even respond with fan-
tastic stories as other Gypsies might; the would-be interlocutor will simply leave without further ado. They must either really have respect for
the questioner or they must be in coercive circumstances to remain. But
if they remain in the conversation, they will then clutch, as if it were a
life buoy, the stubborn leitmotif *žāno gar,* "I don't know," when it is obvious that they do know the answer. "I don't know": among us things
aren't learned that way.

At the same time, everything I wrote at the beginning of the book
shows that the Mānuš are, regardless of what they are doing, telling each
other that they are Mānuš. They are *Cajxi.* How can plenitude be conju-

gated when it is always all or nothing: the Pirdo who wants to be "half Mānuš" is nothing. I have to repeat that silence, this invisible caesura that separates them from other people, links Mānuš to each other. When they leave each other, they don't say good-bye but, and the formula has become so much a habit that it seems the equivalent of a good-bye, *Penā menge či,* "We don't say anything." So that's it: the Mānuš do not indulge in ritual elaborations but they do cultivate a certain tonality, a certain quality of human relationship. The whole of the symbolic apparatus leading to the organization of the world according to the specific and complex characteristics I have described has its starting point in the sorrow caused by the death of a loved one. There's a banal aspect, as the acts of homage for the dead are first a way of treating pain. Anthropology has not been interested in sorrow (an individual affect—which is universal) but in mourning (a social institution—which is specific), that is, in the social treatment of sorrow.

Each death in the Mānuš community, as elsewhere, brings sorrow and mourning. In the course of some funerals, at the moment when the loved one is put in the coffin and then the coffin in the tomb, men and women cry and scream, some rip their clothes and scratch their own faces while their brothers and sisters, unkempt and with their eyes red from sleepless nights, let them do it . . . Then all concerned perform gestures of respect as correctly as they feel they have to. And very quickly shame, modesty—that is, silence—covers up the sound of pain. We have seen how homage to the dead brought about the appearance of a private, intimate, individual sphere. The community, which during periods of mourning seems completely preoccupied with managing the passage of the deceased from presence (all the place he/she was occupying in the horizon of the living, a place that could be tireless, taciturn, or happy) to absence (at first a different mode of presence, an invisible presence, constituted by respect, and then the advent of the individual dead into anonymity and silence), is at the same time and with the same gestures, taking care of the pain of the living. This indeed involves the solicitude of the community toward one of its members who is left alone to experience its sweetness, in the camp, at night, when the survivor unties the scarves or the handkerchiefs where the photographs and keepsakes of the loved one are kept, when the mourner caresses these objects, kisses them, talks to them, when finally she or he falls asleep by repeating the

departed's name or singing the loved one's song . . . Finally also, in the
dialogue with the "poor dead" at the grave sites, the Mānuš speak of the
tenderness that is kept out of public life.

Moments of privileged complicity are not all passed over with silence. Sometimes the Mānuš give in to the gratuitousness that is the privilege of the living—with games, teasing, tall tales, exaggerations.[24] There
were bursts of joy in the olden days "when the horses returned . . ." (We
had put the horses out to pasture at night in a field of grass or clover, we
would tie them with long chains so that they would not get lost. The big
mallet we used to hammer in the metal stake had to be wrapped in cloth
so that the peasants would not hear us, and we went back to the camp
with free hands, walking in a single file between the hedges, sure-footed
in the dark, and with the urge to play till dawn . . .) Today it's "when the
junk trucks return . . ." (In front of the trailers, tables have been set, and
those who have started to eat call upon the others to "come taste this
food!," "come have a glass of wine!" and people go from one table to the
next, comparing the merits of a recipe, and for once men and women
joke together . . .) Then the pure joy of speech resonates with the elated
acceptance of the sole fact of existing. The names of the Mānuš brothers and sisters make space sing, two syllables whose colors tinkle: Ga-
danz! Dadouï! Pounette! . . . And then there are those lists in Mānuš language of all the parts of a car engine where soon the boundary between
knowledge and imagination blurs (*milo,* "the mill," *špricogāria,* "fuel in-
jectors," *trikāri* "accelarator"), and then strings of words created on the
spot bursting out in the course of a conversation: *ganaša,* "bumper,"[25]
*kre dox an u cigania! Na, u cigaria! žāno pu gar: cigania, cigaria, otax
cingāria? Cigaria, cingāria, cingania! Cigania pimaskre! Gar cigāria pimaskre! Gar pimaskri! Ova! Cigania pimaskre!* "So light the *Tziganes,*
no the cigars! I don't know anymore: *Tziganes,* cigars, or turn signals?
Cigars, turn signals, *Tziganes!* Drinking *Tziganes!* Not cigarettes! No,
not something that can be smoked! Yes, drinking *Tziganes!*"[26] These
people who know that things that are important are not apt to be put
into words sometimes seize the pleasure that is thus given to them to say
or show anything they please. The painting on top, the painting of the
surface: Piroto is in the middle of a regular conversation when he suddenly launches into an improvisation made up of onomatopoeia that he
accompanies by miming an accordion player. Bēro, a quinquagenarian

whose wisdom and seriousness all praise, takes advantage of the left-over from some dye, used by his daughter, to color his own chestnut hair and moustache raven black. And Kālo, so punctilious with everything regarding etiquette, politeness between the living, and the respect for the dead, cannot resist the call of castanets as soon as a lively tune comes out of his radio—he has even been known to invent in French dadaist couplets on fifties hits . . . Celebrations of the joy of being in the world, celebrations all the more lively in that they stand out on the background of silence that is Mānuš reality. The discourse-where-the-dead-are makes them Mānuš: it is necessity. The-discourse-between-the-living spreads joy and weaves tenderness between them.

IS NEVER REVEALING WHAT THEY ARE the equivalent of an oath to never let themselves be known? Have they chosen solitude, these people who are always in the midst of others? [27]

A fellow anthropologist once told me that all civilizations have been tempted by silence at one point or another of their existence. Therein might lie the gift the Mānuš make to humanity: taking on to the end the universal temptation of silence about oneself.

It is true that everyone is performing gestures of homage to the dead similar to those the Mānuš make and which make the Mānuš. For instance there are individuals who cease practicing a given activity when the loved one with whom they used to do it dies, or who stop eating or drinking what the departed friend or relative enjoyed, or else stop frequenting the places where the traces of the loved one are still too strong . . . All these marks of respect are universal means of showing the unique character of individual human beings, and thus the irremediable nature of their loss. We do encounter these attitudes in our European societies, and we also encounter them in African societies, as a professor told me after a lecture I gave at the university of Nanterre. However, neither the people mentioned nor anthropologists insist on this. This is because people feel the matter to be private, and no one else's business, and anthropologists focus, in the societies they are studying, on rituals belonging to another sort of dimension: collective, regular, regulated, accompanied with speeches, music, costumes, dances, magical formulas, etc. And thus these gestures of sorrow toward the dead seem incidental to anthropologists, who at times might be performing them themselves.

But not everyone becomes Mānuš. The Mānuš have nothing else. And it is the fact of having nothing else that makes them Mānuš. Silence is the only thing separating them from the rest of humankind. Silence is indeed the only thing they possess.

WHAT ARE THE PEOPLE OF SILENCE SEEKING? A civilization can bask in the spectacle of its own glory, narcissistically admire its own ceremonies and works. What are these works for the Mānuš? The temptation of silence can also be a communion with nature transcending the works of human beings, it can mean choosing kinship with trees, rivers, horses, lizards. It has to be silence because it is language that divides things. Alain Borer, in *Rimbaud en Abyssinie,* speaks of some of the inhabitants of Ogaden,[28] whom he could barely make out amidst the rocks and stones where they were squatting.[29] I remember that after my first encounter with the Mānuš on the shores of the Allier, I wrote in my notebook: " . . . men who resembled trees more than they did present-day urban dwellers." But perhaps it was the distance of the gaze that made Borer see the "Ogadines" as in harmony with stones, sun, the sand. And perhaps it is the distance of time that makes me too see the Mānuš of the wagons as in harmony with the world.

Moršela, Kāri, Kālo, Lebo, Bēro, Butsāri, Nīni , Nelo, Drāka—all are aware that they do not fish and hunt the same way Gadzos do. Mānuš wander the fields alone or with a Mānuš companion that is either a human being or an animal. They travel roads and paths looking out for *cajxi.* They squat by a fire at night. And then there are those horses answering to their names, dogs understanding without the need to utter an order, crows and ravens with whom they are conversing. But just as they can feel their link with nature so perfectly, the Mānuš cannot forget that around them—how can I put it?—trains are running in the plain, mechanical harvesters slay a deluge of flowers, passersby cross streets, invisible waves crisscross the sky . . .[30]

Photographs

1.

3.

4.

5.

6.

8.

9.

10.

11.

12.

14.

16.

17.

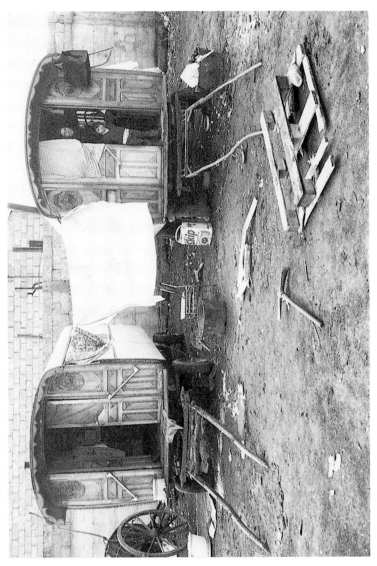

FIVE

Commentary

It seems to me that the approach I have used in this book negates two
types of discourse on the Gypsies.

1. The discourse that makes of the Gypsies an exogenous entity, this
either by seeing them as a more or less exotic, a more or less "domi-
nated" "minority," or by designating them as one of the groups that,
through a centrifugal movement specific to Western societies, find themselves shunted to the margins. This approach defines Gypsies in terms
of "deviance," "social handicap," etc.

I have often been told that what I am describing are only fragments,
and that what I have seen is only the ruin of Mānuš society and culture,
a society and culture whose erosion is in the process of being completed
through contact with ours. This view doubly contradicts what I have en-
deavored to show.

Firstly, that view presumes an ideal state, an "authentic" Mānuš identity, which it places on the outside of the society, where we encounter the
bearers of this identity, outside of space and time. Yet there is nothing
to indicate that Mānuš culture was fundamentally different in the past
from what it is in the present (by this I do not mean that it is immutable
but rather that it is an ongoing process of creation): the Mānuš made
their appearance in the midst of Western societies, they constitute themselves within them. There is no point for an anthropologist in recon-
structing an original state of "before colonization."

And then, secondly, that view leads to denying the creativity of the
Mānuš and turns them into the clumsy and unfortunate inheritors of a
"tradition" that no longer belongs to them, and that in any case they
would not know how to keep alive. In contrast, my research highlights
the inventiveness of the Mānuš, the part left to individual creativity and
imagination, along with the possibility of variation and innovation. If

Mānuš rituals are fluid, nonuniversal, imperfectly codified, it is not because of accident or clumsiness but because of their properties.

2. The second discourse negated by this book is one that lets itself be
caught by Mānuš modes of expression, a discourse carrying the idea that
if they don't say anything it must be because they have nothing to say,
that if it appears that we are dealing with nothingness, it must be because
there is indeed nothing. The reason for the large place I give to description, a place that at the close of this book seems to me still perhaps not
large enough, is to show that yes, of course, there is something here.

The Mānuš could never be associated with vacuity; they live in the
midst of a world that is full. The introduction of void is that which constitutes them. When we know that any object might be *mullo,* and that
this cannot be seen, that any place could be a *mūlengri placa,* and that
this cannot be seen, that any attitude can be a homage to the dead, but
that nothing makes it possible to know this for sure, we then know that
all things can be at once what they seem to be and something else. *Cajxi.*
A Mānuš can be at once a Mānuš and an ordinary individual, a person just
like everyone else. Only the dead are Mānuš who can only be Mānuš. But
of them, very soon, nothing more can be said.

NOTES

CHAPTER ONE

1. The author uses the French generic term "Tsiganes." I could not translate the generic name by "Roma" or "Romani," the preferred terms of American groups, for reasons explained below, and thus translated it as "Gypsy." Patrick Williams (personal communication) notes that there is no word in French designating all the groups of so-called *Tsiganes* corresponding to the way these groups name themselves. In French, the term "Gitan," in ordinary language, and "Tsigane," in scholarly works, are the two generic terms used most frequently. They do carry a number of clichés and prejudices. This does not prevent members of these groups, such as the Mānuš, from sometimes using these words, particularly when conversing with outsiders, that is, with Gadzos. But among themselves the Mānuš call themselves "Mānuš." They do not use the term "Roma," used by organizations working for the cultural and political advancement of Tsiganes groups. The term "rom" (both in the singular and plural modes) does exist in the Mānuš dialect; it has two meanings, indicating either "husband" or a male in general, whether Gadzo or Mānuš. For the Mānuš the terms "Rom" or "Roma" used generically designate those they uniformly call "Hungaria" or in French "Hongrois" [Hungarian], that is, the actual Rom groups present in France (it is thought that the Mānuš refer to them as "Hungarians" because the first Rom group the Mānuš came into contact with were the Lovara Rom, originating from Hungary). The Mānuš do not refer to themselves as "Rom" and correct any person who calls them by that name. — *Trans.*

2. In French society, Mānuš are referred to as "Manouches." In the French text, the author has used "Mānuš" as a noun, but the dictates of French grammar forced him to keep "manouche" as an adjective. As English allows me to use Mānuš as an adjective, I have forgone the use of "manouche" altogether. The Mānuš themselves refer to non-Roma as "Gadjé," which is rendered in English as "Gadzo." The author's original footnote follows. — *Trans.*

Gadjé: meaning "non-Tziganes." I chose this transcription because it is the most common one. From a phonological viewpoint, "Gāže" better renders Mānuš pronunciation. I am using "Mānuš" rather than "Manouche" to respect the name that the women and men of whom I speak about give themselves. I am using "manouche" when dealing with an adjective within a French phrase.

3. An oddity has to be noted: while "our" Mānuš introduce themselves as "*Am* Mānuš," their cousins from Germanic territories prefer to say "*Am* Sinte."

CHAPTER TWO

1. *Boulles,* or *pétanque,* is a southern French game similar to the Italian game of bocce, except that metal balls instead of wooden ones are used. The ball fills the palm of a hand, and the aim is to throw the ball as close as possible to a smaller one with as few throws as possible and while trying to dislodge opponents' balls.— *Trans.*

2. Django Reinhardt has become among his people as well as among the Gadzo such a well-known hero primarily of course because of the power of his artistic creativity. But if it had not been for recordings of his works, for their diffusion and successive re-recordings over the years due to his popularity with a non- Gypsy public, the Mānuš community would not have been able to claim Django Reinhardt's work and use it as its emblem as it does today. In terms of Mānuš attitudes toward the dead, the posthumous fate of Reinhardt's work among the Mānuš seems even more exceptional than his career and life (Williams 1991a).

3. An Alsatian writer, Marie-Paul Dollé, author of the book *Les Tsiganes manouches* (1980), had troubles with some families because he had used photographs of their deceased as illustrations. See Joly and Steinberger 1980.

4. Abbé Joseph Valet, author of *Vocabulaire des Manouches d'Auvergne* [Lexicon of the Manouches of Auvergne] ([1971] 1986), tells that the family of a recently deceased Mānuš went to retrieve from his pickup truck the recordings they had done with him so as to destroy them. Today, the families ask that those tapes, or copies of them, be given to them . . .

5. The English expression "it comes back to me, does it come back to you?" renders that thought. I have kept the awkward form used by the author in French to maintain his argument.— *Trans.*

6. The French expressions used by the author are ungrammatical in French but they do exist in English.— *Trans.*

7. *Vocabulaire des Manouches d'Auvergne:* "*Ēra: unti vel tut ēra pur māre dine mūlenge:* have honor for our poor defunct; *i tut i ēra fur menge:* you have honor for us (you are treating us well); *i tut kek ēra mange:* you have no respect for me. *Tengrōva:* I think, *tenkō man:* I am thinking; *tengel man:* I remember, *tengrel man als:* I will always remember."

8. The expression was stated in French and not in Mānuš: *et toute sa race!*

9. In French, *le revenant* is a noun that means literally "the one who comes back."— *Trans.*

10. See chap. 4.

11. Loli's narrative [words in bold are French words interspersed by the narrator in her Mānuš text.— *Trans.*]:

> *I mōlo umes an mur vāgo, mur karavana . . . Is men graj an ko cajto. Mur* **belle-mère** *is* **en face** *mande . . . O phenum? Me an mur tin vāgo, mur tin čāve soven, un mur rom is ani virta te pijel mōl* **parce que** *mur rom pijel gar . . .*
>
> *Me umes krat kake kōkri, mur* **belle-mère en face,** *mur tin čāve soven. Me angrō man an mur spīglo. Mur* **belle-mère** *del gōji mange. Mur* **belle-mère** *kras man kek dar. Mur* **belle-mère:** *"Ap Loli! Tēle mit tur čāvencax! ǯā an u vāgo fun i Pato!"*
>
> **Bon.** *O krōva? Me lō mire čāven, ǯā ani vāgo fun i Pato.*

Ax anle an u vāgo fun i Pato, u vāgo vias bobardemen fun u bax! Ta!
Dijam gōji! Un phandam u vūdar cu, liam menge kotax kast, daram dox,
un u murš viansle gar . . . I brī dar!

One time we were in my trailer, my old trailer. My mother-in-law's trailer
was facing mine . . . What did I say? Me in my little trailer. My small children were sleeping, and my man was in the bar drinking wine, because he
doesn't like wine, right!

So I was all alone and my mother-in-law's trailer was facing mine, my
little children asleep. I was combing my hair in front of the mirror. My
mother-in-law starts to scream to me. My mother-in-law did not frighten
me. My mother-in-law: "Come Loli! Come quick with your children! Let's
go to Pato's trailer!"

Well. What did I do? I grabbed my kids and we went to Pato's trailer.

As soon as we got into Pato's trailer, it was bombarded with pebbles!
We screamed! Ta! We had closed the door, we grabbed a stick, we were
very frightened, and the men were not coming . . . That was a great fright!

12. The French word *décalage* has no exact equivalent in English. It can refer
to anything "out of sinc" in time or space, as for instance in jet lag, or a schedule
change, or the loss of synchronicity between different parts of an engine. The author uses it figuratively to express the gaps the Mānuš create in time and in space
so as to construct their own universe within those gaps. Paradoxically, the universe thus created in the interstices of the dominant one becomes itself a totality.
I have thus I translated each instance of *décalage* in terms of the textual context
but have added the French word in parenthesis.—*Trans.*

13. *Vocabulaire des Manouches d'Auvergne:* "*cajxi:* signs on the road. *Kredum
cajxi ap u drom, i buco graza un zanta pre:* I made signs on the road, a tuft of grass
with sand over it."

CHAPTER THREE

1. *Gens du Voyage* literally means "People of the Travel" or "Travel People,"
echoing for instance "The Forest People" or "the French People" and conveying
the meaning that "travel" is the country of the Mānuš.—*Trans.*

2. In this quote and elsewhere in Mānuš-language quotes in this book, words
in bold are French words interspersed by the narrator in the Mānuš text.—*Trans.*

3. English word now part of the French language meaning a travel trailer or
RV.—*Trans.*

4. The French term is "forain industriel," meaning an individual owning and
managing one stand or more at fairs all year round, this in contrast to Mānuš, who
might work fairs a part of the year and whose stands are more rudimentary
(Patrick Williams, personal communication).—*Trans.*

5. On the Travelers' argot, see chap. 4, note 9.

6. *Rom* ("man") is here used by Mānuš to designate other Mānuš when they
are not referring to them by their names. There is a nuance of respect in the word.
Kāre dox u rom te vel te xal mancax! "Call the man to come eat with me!"

7. *Fêtier:* French word that can be loosely translated by the English word
"carny."—*Trans.*

8. Duville is a Mānuš family name belonging to Mānuš different from those of

Auvergne. The Auvergne Mānuš use it as a generic name without regard to whether the people they so designate really bear this particular family name (Patrick Williams, personal communication). — *Trans.*

9. "To peel" a hedgehog means, once the animal has been shaved, to get rid of remaining quills by burning them with fire and then scraping them with a knife and to get rid of skin on its stomach by peeling it.

10. The author uses the French abbreviation in common use in France: *SDF,* or "Sans Domicile Fixe," literally "without a fixed domicile." — *Trans.*

11. Literally "false paths": these are paths or roads leading only to woods or fields. — *Trans.*

12. Predari 1841, cited in Piasere 1985, 136.

CHAPTER FOUR

1. Nēlo narrates the following:

J'étais jeune marié, ... *Umes freš romdino. Is i menši mancax, is mur romni. žum paš u lumpomāno , rodum brī tin vāgo— une poussette—, ginum ki šeza, i tausto ginum la.*

ž'am bāro drom, un umes kīno. Un is man duj žūkle. Allez, španova kol duj tin žūkle an. Kek graj is man. Un mur romni helfreli i šeza. U kuč Tata (xoxō gar ap leste!) islo glan mit u vāgo. Tajl is bārga tele, bārga pre ... Tajl vel i brī desenda kake! helfrāsi an i romni dox! un i tin žūkle carden. Tellement ke carden kol tin žūkle, mukasli i šeza te žāl ... i romni mukasli. Kaj flīgo me? Krat an i tāla tēle! I šeza is ap mande, u čiben, čeli vesal pre!

I was a newlywed ... My parents were with me, so was my wife. I went to the junk store, I looked for a little carriage, a big one, a baby carriage. I paid one thousand francs for it.

We had a long road ahead and I was tired. I had two dogs. So I hitch my two small dogs. I did not have a horse. And my wife helps to push the carriage. My late father (let me not lie when speaking of him!) was ahead with the wagon. We had to go up and down hills ... And there was this slope we had to go down, huge! Ah, my wife was pushing with all her might! And the two dogs were pulling. They pulled so hard she let go of the carriage ... My wife let it go. And where did I fly? All the way down! The carriage fell upside down on me, the bedding, all the dishes on top!

2. "Bohemian" should be taken here with the connotation of "tramp." — *Trans.*

3. A "tube" is a small panel truck. — *Trans.*

4. Figures from INSEE.

5. 1962: 508,672; 1968: 544,568; 1975: 545,629; 1982: 595,812; 1990: 598,493 (INSEE).

6. In 1962: 182,742 inhabitants aged twenty-five years or less; 69,790 older than sixty-five. In 1975: 171,122 younger than twenty years old; 111,720 older than sixty. In 1990: 147,902 younger than twenty years old; 124,808 older than sixty.

The age groups counted by the INSEE changed somewhat over the years, but this does not negate the aging of the population, a trend even sharper in the *département* of Creuse.

7. The post office functions as a bank in France.—*Trans.*

8. Only a comparison of the demographics of Mānuš families with that of the population as a whole seems to explain this deterioration. We do not have specific and complete statistics for the "nomads" or *Tsiganes* and even less for the Mānuš of the Central Massif (or elsewhere). It is however possible to come up with a pertinent approximation by looking at the figures in the Bideberry report commissioned by the prime minister on June 30, 1980, and which did a census of holders of *carnets de circulation.*

Less than sixteen years old: 47 percent (for the whole of the French population, this ratio is 27 percent), from sixteen to sixty-five years old: 51 percent (whole of the French population: 59 percent), older than sixty-five: 2 percent (whole of the French population: 14 percent). The demography of the region accentuates the national trend of the aging of the population, which itself reflects the lowering of the birth rate, even when taking into account that there are more elderly people in the villages and hamlets than in urban centers. Mānuš adolescents are over-flowing with life and the children are so alert and active that they always give the impression of being more numerous than in reality.

9. "Traveler" argot: *Avant j'le dikavais tous les soirs dans la virta,* "Before, I saw him every evening in the bar." The Gypsy verb *dikhav,* "I see" (Gypsy verbs don't have the infinitive form), is conjugated as if it were a French verb in the first person present tense: *kerav,* "I make," is conjugated into *je kérav, je kéravais, j'ai kérav,* etc. [I make, I will make, I have made, etc.]; *marav,* "I hit," is conjugated *je marav, j'ai marav,* etc. The following is the same sentence in French, Mānuš, and Traveler argot [and then in English]:

Je vais avec mon oncle voir le gendarme qui a l'habitude de remplir nos papiers.
žō mit mur kak paš ko klisto k ilo siklo te krel māre papīrja.
Jm'en vas avec l'oncle vers le klisto qui kérav toujours nos papiers.
[I am going with my uncle to see the gendarme who habitually fills out our papers.]

The syntax is French, and so is most of the vocabulary. Exotic words come from Gypsy dialects, mainly Mānuš. For some people this argot is reduced simply to an accent or to using French turns of phrases that are "incorrect" or archaic and which end up becoming characteristic and function as signs of recognition:

[Argot] *Que j'meure à l'instant si j'le marav pas!*
[French] *Que je meure sur le champ si je ne le frappe pas!*
[Let me die instantly if I don't hit him.]

[Argot] *Trop bon il est mon p'tit!*
[French] *Il est si beau mon fils.*
[So beautiful is my son.]

[Argot] *I-z-ont venus tous ses parents vers elle, quelle contentesse!*
[French] *Tous ses parents sont venus la voir chez elle, quelle joie!*
[All her relatives came to see her at her home, what joy!]

[Argot]   *I-z-étions bleus, schtrack!*
[French] *Ils étaient ivres, raides!*
[They were dead drunk!]

(See P. Williams 1988, 381–413.)

10. Alain Reyniers (1992, 242) met Mānuš families who were no longer using their language for daily interactions. The only circumstance in which they still spoke Mānuš was when visiting gravesites and talking to the dead.

11. And yet, as I leaf through the pages of these calendars, I rediscover on the date of July 29, 1990, a quote from a film critic from an article about Andrej Wajda, which perfectly renders the impression that I now feel during funerals when looking at the nieces and nephews of the one we are burying: "Time, yet caught yesterday in memory's nets, again finds its renovating force. It has taken the side of innocence and joy against that of resentment and sadness."

12. Looking at the map of the spread of Pentecostalism among the Gypsies of Europe, where it has not met with the same success everywhere, it is difficult to propose only one explanation for its spread (see Williams 1993 for a survey of the various possible explanations for this success).

The development of this messianic movement among Gypsies is of course linked to a certain state of the relation Gypsy–non-Gypsy. The Gypsies became Pentecostal when the Gadzos attempted to create associations to deal with "the Gypsy problem," when Gadzos became "scientifically" interested in the Gypsies and published books on their "customs," when they wanted to "let the Gypsies speak" . . . Conversions also took place a few years after the Gadzos decided to permanently get rid of the Gypsies as a separate entity.

Based on the reading of the trajectory of a young Mānuš convert, I have attempted to offer an answer to the question "what transformation does conversion to Pentecostalism bring into the life of its Gypsy members?" (Williams 1991c).

13. According to William Samarin, Pentecostals conceive of speaking in tongue as being baptized by the Holy Ghost. It is called "glossolalia" by linguists, who define it as "a meaningless but phonologically structured human utterance believed by the speaker to be a real language but bearing no systematic resemblance to any natural language, living or dead" (Samarin 1972, 2, cited in Courtine 1988, 20).

14. Pentecostal prayers and laying of hands (done most often by the preachers) are mediating acts making miraculous healing possible. Healing, whether of oneself or of a family member, very often provides the impetus for conversions. It is at least in this manner that things are presented in converted Gypsies' public testimonials.

15. Matéo Maximoff, a Rom Kalderaš pastor, introduced this theme in 1966 in an article he wrote for *Vie et lumière,* the trimonthly newsletter of the Gypsy evangelical mission.

16. Maryse Delisle, who worked among the Mānuš of the Parisian region, perfectly describes this feeling when she writes about "a religious double of profane life."

17. One sometimes has the impression that, as required by the conquest of the world of the Gadzos, the Mānuš leave to others the job of defining the universe, that is, the universe as it would be without people. God, the stars, the cycles of

the seasons . . . all these are the purview of the Gadzos. This hypothesis could be extended from the Mānuš to other Gypsies. Leonardo Piasere (1985), writing about the Slovensko Roma, argues that God the Creator and all of his saints honored by the Roma belong to the *gažikano* domain (that is, the Gadzo domain, the relation with the Gadzos), and he drew my attention to an episode in Jan Yoors' (1990) autobiography: having to swear an oath in the midst of particularly serious circumstances, a character opposes "the God of the Gadzos" to the *Mūle des Lovara.*

18. For an example of this sort of denunciation, albeit one more nuanced than that expounded by certain preachers, see the bulletin of the Mission évangélique tzigane, *Vie et lumière,* no. 85, "Les Tsiganes et la superstition," no. 91, "Le peuple man-ouche," and no. 103, "De la magie . . . à la Bible."

19. Is this the case for all Mānuš? (It is useless to ask the question for "Gypsies" in general as there are too many differences in their attitudes toward the dead).

The scene is a Paris suburb in the winter of 1988 in the evangelical hall of Livry-Gargan, where a preacher is preaching fire and brimstone. For a whole hour and half, in a language that speaks to the Mānuš because it is that of their everyday life, he evokes the horrors and the sufferings of hell. Then at the end of this terrible depiction, the preacher reveals his proselytizing aim. Those who refuse to follow the word of God, those who refuse conversion, will experience these eternal torments. The two preachers then invite the audience to ask questions. There is a moment of hesitation: the listeners probably need a few minutes to recover from all those frightful visions. Finally a young girl, about seventeen years old, for whom perhaps Pentecostalism has been her only religion, as her parents were already converted before she was born, raises her hand and asks, "And our poor departed then?" There is confusion and embarrassment on the stage. The preachers consult each other . . . After some fuzzy explanations they finally find the answer: those who did not know of the word of God are not implicated, they did not have that choice at the time they were living.

20. Claude Lévi-Strauss (1963 [1955], 338–39):

Towards the end of the morning we were working our way round a big bush when we suddenly found ourselves face to face with two natives who were travelling in the opposite direction. The older of the two was about forty. Dressed in a tattered pair of pyjamas, he wore his hair down to his shoulders. The other had his hair cut short and was entirely naked, save for the little cornet of straw which covered his penis. On his back, in a basket of green palm-leaves tied tightly round the creature's body, was a large harpy-eagle. Trussed like a chicken, it presented a lamentable appearance, despite its grey-and-white-stripped plumage and its head, with powerful yellow beak, and crown of feathers standing on end. Each of the two natives carried a bow and arrows.

From the conversation which followed between them and Abaitara it emerged that they were, respectively, the chief of the village we were hoping to get to, and his right-hand man. They had gone on ahead of the other villagers, who were wandering somewhere in the forest. The whole party was bound for the Machado with the object of paying their visit,

promised a year previously, to Pimenta Bueno. The eagle was intended as
a present for their hosts. All this did not really suit us, for we wanted not
only to meet them, but to meet them in their own village. It was only after
they had been promised a great many gifts when they got to the Porquinho
camp that they agreed, with the greatest reluctance, to turn in their tracks,
march back with us, and make us welcome in their village. This done, we
would set off, all together, by river. Once we had agreed on all this, the
trussed eagle was jettisoned without ceremony by the side of a stream
where it seemed inevitable that it would very soon either die of hunger or
be eaten alive by ants. Nothing more was said about it during the next
fifteen days, except that a summary "death certificate" was pronounced:
"He's dead, that eagle." The two Kawahib vanished into the forest to tell
their families of our arrival, and we continued on our way.

The incident of the eagle set me thinking. Several ancient authors re-
late that the Tupi breed eagles, feed them on monkeys' flesh, and periodi-
cally strip them of their feathers. Rondon had noted this among the Tupi-
Kawahib, and other observers reported it among certain tribes of the
Xingu and the Araguaya. It was not surprising, therefore, that a Tupi-
Kawahib group should have preserved the custom, nor that the eagle,
which they considered as their most precious property, should be taken
with them as a gift, if these natives had really made up their minds (as I
was beginning to suspect, and as I later verified) to leave their village for
good and throw in their lot with civilization. But that only made more in-
comprehensible their decision to abandon the eagle to its pitiable fate. Yet
the history of colonization, whether in South America or elsewhere, is
marked by these radical renunciations of traditional values and repudia-
tions of a style of life, in which the loss of certain elements at once causes
all other elements to be marked down: perhaps I had just witnessed a
characteristic instance of this phenomenon.

21. The story of the Mānuš, the Pirdo, and the hedgehog lies at the point of
equilibrium where genetic necessity is reaffirmed ("it's in the blood") and social
implications are brought out ("don't become a Pirdo, my brother!")—at the point
of rupture where silence becomes discourse? Moršela does not explain, even
though he shows how things must be transmitted. He does this without any di-
dacticism, just a bit of a story in between two games of *pétanque*. But already, because he knows how to distance himself from the feeling of necessity, even if it is
only to remind us of it (and this perhaps because he is too friendly with the anthropologist), he has a foot in the universe of discourse. As Todorov has noted,
"it seems that the man who assumes a discourse on religion takes the first step toward the abandonment of religious discourse itself" (Todorov 1984, 190).

22. This is a well-known tale. An art lover buys a painting. She looks at it so
much that the feeling grows in her that beneath this landscape (in some other ver-
sions it's a portrait) there lies another landscape (or behind this portrait, another
face). She is more and more fascinated by this landscape (or face) she cannot see.
Finally she can no longer stand it and scrapes the surface painting. She continues
to admire this new landscape (or face) that she herself has uncovered. But she
contemplates it so much a feeling grows in her that beneath this landscape (or
face) there is yet another even more fascinating . . . But what if there was nothing?

And yet, this is not the story that was constantly on my mind while writing this book, but rather a scene from Frederico Fellini's film *Roma*. Faience frescoes in the ancient Roman substrate are discovered in the course of work in the subway tunnels beneath the city. Brought to light are personages caught in their dialogue with eternity, but their images fade away as they are exposed.

23. For Miles Davis, "inside a melody, there's another melody. That's the one we have to find" (cited in Simon 1991, 3).

24. *Ax žalso rāti te vajtrel peske graj, u phūro Kuna, is les mit jek tikni reca. žalsi glan i reca, un jop palal. žāne gar o phenelo ko phūro kāva? Ax nakheli i reca paš u hēko un deli goji coin! coin! coin! Akelo u nīglo! Ako mōlo ke krasli kake— coin! coin! coin!—acasli jek nīglo!* (At night when he used to bring his horses to pasture, old Kuna would bring along a small duck. The duck walked ahead, and he followed behind. You know what that old guy said? When the duck would pass a bush it would start to scream "coin! coin! coin! Here's a hedgehog!" Each time it would do this—"coin! coin! coin!"—each time he had found a hedgehog!)

žānen gar čovāle o phenas mange vavax mōlo o Fāni? žālo gar budax te mangel jop! Un šafrelo gar. Či! Čelo dīves pašemen! Jop phenelo, o Fāni! žūkel i leste. Jop čivelo duj müzeti ap i men fun ko žūkel un bičelo les ap o rojmo . . . Goželo žūkel! An ki müzeta čivelo dren u lolo kūpro, an i vavax müzeta o žilto kūpro! (Do you guys know what the Fani told me the other day? He doesn't go out to peddle anymore! He doesn't work! Nothing! In bed all day long! That's what he told me, the Fani. He has a dog. On this dog, he puts two bags around his neck and he sends him to the dump. What a clever dog! In one bag he puts red copper, and in the other, yellow copper!)

25. *ganaša:* the jaw

26. Word play on *cingari*, "turn signal"; *cigani*, "Tzigane"; *cigāri*, "cigar" (actually a word invented on the spot); and on *pimaskri*, "cigarette," and *pimaskro*, "drinker."

27. Chateaubriand, in the April 1822 chapter of his *Memoirs*, where he was narrating his experiences among the Niagara Indians, wrote this about the "peoples of solitude":

> In what regards the dead, it is easy to find to find motives for the savage's attachment to sacred relics. Civilized nations are able to preserve the memory of their country by means of the mnemonics of literature and the arts: they have cities, palaces, towers, columns, obelisks; they have the track of the plough in fields once cultivated; their names are carved in marble and brass, their actions recorded in the chronicles.
>
> [The people of solitude have none of these:] their names are not written upon the trees; their huts, built in a few hours, disappear in a few moments; the butt of their ploughing only grazes the ground, and is not able even to raise a furrow. Their traditional songs perish with the last memory which retains them, and die away with the last voice which repeats them . . . Take away from savages the bones of their fathers, and you take away their history, their laws, and their very gods; you rob those men, in the future generations, of the proofs of their existence . . . (Chateaubriand 1902: 1, 231) [I have substituted the segment in brackets for the one written by Chateaubriand's 1902 translator, as it deviated too much from the original.— *Trans.*]

28. Ogaden was an Ethiopian kingdom at the time of Rimbaud's nineteenth-century visit in what was then known to Europeans as Abyssinia (Patrick Williams, personal communication).— *Trans.*

29. Alain Borer (1984, 70–71) writes:

Contemplating this rocky landscape stretching beyond my field of vision, my gaze was suddenly caught by something standing out from the hill facing me. By focusing carefully on that spot I made out a squatting man, whose brown clothes and immobility made him almost impossible to distinguish from, [in Rimbaud's words], "the steppe of tall grass and rocky crags." Through the zoom lens of our camera we saw between the bushes and the rocks several men and a child, all motionless in the heat. These were the "Ogadines" described by Rimbaud: "their daily routine consists of squatting in groups . . . they are completely inactive." I automatically looked at my watch: it was eleven thirty in the morning . . . What was I doing last week? I was running through the suffocating corridors of a subway station. It was hard to grasp that these *Ogadines* were our contemporaries. I saw them like Rimbaud did, and probably the way they have always been. They did not give the impression of the misery found in large cities: they did not conjure up the third world but another world. This might be "real life," original, essentially linked to the earth with which they blended, freed of all superfluous cares and new needs created by the time-bound society that was looking at them through our big optical apparatus . . .

30. Jean Grenier (1961, 153): "Sometimes, stopping my weaving of a spider web, I went to the window of my prison to look at . . . —how can I put it?—trains running on the plain, mechanical harvesters slaying a deluge of flowers, passersby crossing streets, waves crisscrossing the sky . . ."

REFERENCES

Barthélémy, A., and Joseph Valet. 1975. *I muleskri plaxta: Le drap du mort.* *Études tsiganes* 21 (1): 1–3.

Baubérot, Jean. 1988. *Le protestantisme doit-il mourir?* Paris: Seuil.

Bideberry, P. 1981. Extraits du rapport sur la situation des "Gens du Voyage" et les mesures pour l'améliorer. *Études tsiganes* 27 (2): 1–17.

Bizeul, Daniel. 1987. Des Voyageurs sur un terrain spécialisé: Sort commun et différenciations. *Études tsiganes* 33 (4): 19–26.

Borer, Alain. 1984. *Rimbaud en Abyssinie.* Paris: Seuil.

Bourdin, Alain. 1984. Tsiganes, politiques sociales et terrains de stationnement. *Études tsiganes* 30 (2): 22–28.

Calvet G., F. Delvoye, and M. Labalette. 1970. Abrégé grammatical du dialecte mānuš. *Études tsiganes* 26 (1): 69–79.

Chateaubriand, François René, vicomte de. 1902. *Memoirs.* 6 vols. Translated by Alexander Teixeira de Mattos. London: Freemantle and Co.

Courtine, Jean-Jacques. 1988. Les silences de la voix: Histoire et structure des glossolalies. In "Les glossolalies." Special issue, *Langages* 91: 5–25.

Daval, M., and D. Joly. 1979a. Mode de vie, coutumes, traditions. In "Les Tsiganes d'Alsace." Special issue, *Saisons d'Alsace* 23 (67): 25–32.

———. 1979b. La langue des Tsiganes. In "Les Tsiganes d'Alsace." Special issue, *Saisons d'Alsace* 23 (67): 64–78.

Delisle, Maryse. 1985–86. Le pentecôtisme chez les Tsiganes: Être "chrétien" chez des Sinte-Manouches et Voyageurs. Master's thesis (*thèse de troisième cycle*). University of Paris X-Nanterre.

Doerr, C. 1982. *Où vas-tu Manouche?* Bordeaux: Wallada.

Dollé, Marie-Paul. 1970. Symbolique de la mort en milieu tsigane. *Études tsiganes* 26 (4): 4–15.

———. 1980. *Les Tsiganes manouches.* Sand, France: Marie-Paul Dollé.

Erdös, C. 1959. La notion de *mulo* ou de mort-vivant et le culte des morts chez les Tsiganes hongrois. *Études tsiganes* 5(1): 1–9.

Glize, Richard. 1989. L'Église évangélique tzigane comme voie possible d'un engagement culturel nouveau. In *Tsiganes: Identité, évolution,* edited by Patrick Williams, 433–43. Paris: Études tsiganes-Syros Alternatives.

Goubet, M., and J. L. Roucolle. 1984. *Population et société françaises, 1945–1984.* Paris: Sirey.

Grenier, Jean. 1961. La rose sans épines. In *Inspirations méditerranéennes.* Paris: Gallimard.

Jakobson, Roman. 1976. *Six leçons sur le son et le sens.* Paris: Éditions de Minuit.

Jean, D. 1970. Glossaire du gadškeno mānuš. *Études tsiganes* 26(1): 2–69.

Joly, D., and R. Steinberger. 1980. Lorsque les Sinte contestent l'ethnologue. *Monde gitan* 55: 11–14.

Lanternari, V. 1983. *Les mouvements religieux des peuples opprimés.* Paris: La Découverte-Maspero.

Le Cossec, C. 1991. *Mon aventure chez les Tsiganes.* Soignolles, France: C. Le Cossec.

Lévi-Strauss, Claude. 1963. *Tristes Tropiques.* Translated by John Russell. New York: Atheneum.

———. 1958. *Anthropologie structurale.* Paris: Plon.

Liégeois, J. P. 1983. *Tsiganes.* Paris: La Découverte-Maspero.

Malinowski, Bronislaw. 1968. Le mythe dans la psychologie primitive. In *Trois essais sur la vie sociale des primitifs.* Translated by S. Jankélévitch. Paris: Payot.

Martinez, N. 1979. Mythe et réalités du phénomène "Tzigane," Ethno-sociologie des nomades et nomades sédentarisés de France. 4. vols. Ph.D. diss. (*thèse de doctorat d'État*). University of Montpellier III.

Matzen, R. 1979. Histoire d'un *mulo. Saisons d'Alsace* 23 (67): 148–52.

Maximoff, Matéo. 1966. Parallèles des lois de l'Ancien Testament et des lois des Rom. *Vie et lumière* 26: 24–25.

Mission évangélique tsigane. 1985. De la magie . . . à la Bible. *Vie et lumière* 103: n.p.

———. 1979. Les Tsiganes et la superstition. *Vie et lumière* 85: n.p.

———. 1981. Le peuple man-ouche. *Vie et lumière* 91: n.p.

Okely, Judith. 1983. *The Traveller-Gypsies.* Cambridge: Cambridge University Press.

Piasere, Leonardo. 1985. *Mare Roma: Catégories humaines et structure sociale: Une contribution à l'ethnologie tsigane.* Paris: Études et documents balkaniques et méditerranéens.

———. 1995. I segni "segreti" degli Zingari. *La Ricerca folklorica* 31: 83–105.

Predari, F. 1841. *Origine e vicende dei Zingari.* Milano: Lampato.

Rao, A. 1976. Les Tsiganes sinte du Polygone. *Revue des sciences sociales de la France de l'Est* 5: 182–201.

Reyniers, Alain. 1988. Les "compagnons du buisson": Le hérisson au pays des Tsiganes. In "Des hommes et des bêtes." *Terrain* 10: 63–73.

———. 1992. La roue et la pierre: Contributions anthropo-historique à la connaissance de la production sociale et économique des Tsiganes. 2 vols. Ph.D. diss. (*thèse de doctorat*). University of Paris V.

Reyniers, Alain, and Patrick Williams. 1990. Permanence tsigane et politique de sédentarisation dans la France de l'après-guerre. In "Identité et sociétés nomades." Special issue, *Études rurales* 120: 89–106.

Samarin, William. 1972. *Tongues of Men and Angels: The Religious Language of Pentecostalism.* New York: Macmillan.

Simon, Jean-René. 1991. Introduction to a special issue of *Jazz Magazine* on the occasion of the death of Miles Davis. (Simon does not provide the source for the quote.)

Smith, P. 1968. Mythe: 1. Approche ethno-sociologique. In *Encyclopaedia universalis.* Paris: 527–28.

Todorov, Tzvetan. 1987. *The Conquest of America: The Question of the Other.* Translated by Richard Howard. New York: Harper Torchbooks.

Valet, Joseph. 1971. L'environnement du stationnement: La situation en Auvergne. *Études tsiganes* 27 (4): 54–55.

―――. 1972a. *Me am trin nebudi:* Nous sommes trois cousins. *Études tsiganes* 28 (3): 1–3.

―――. 1972b. Le racisme anti-gitan. *Monde gitan* 23: 1–6.

―――. 1975. *O divio Gadžo. Études tsiganes* 21 (4): 1–3.

―――. 1978. La langue des Manouches. *Études tsiganes* 24 (1): 25–28.

―――. 1984a. *Grammaire du manouche d'Auvergne.* Clermont-Ferrand, France: Joseph Valet.

―――. 1984b. *Contes manouches I (Les soeurs Warner).* Clermont-Ferrand, France: Joseph Valet.

―――. 1985. *Contes manouches II (Antoinette Renard).* Clermont-Ferrand, France: Joseph Valet.

―――. 1986 [1971]. *Vocabulaire des Manouches d'Auvergne.* Clermont-Ferrand, France: Joseph Valet.

―――. 1988. *Contes Manouches.* Clermont-Ferrand, France: Joseph Valet.

―――. 1989. Les dialectes du *sinto-manouche:* Caractéristiques générales et différences. In *Tsiganes: Identité, évolution,* edited by Patrick Williams, 309–14. Paris: Études tsiganes-Syros Alternatives.

Williams, Patrick. 1986. Storia del Mānuš, del *Pirdo* e del porcospino. *Lacio Drom* 22(1): 2–22.

―――. 1988. Langue tsigane: Le jeu romanes. In *Vingt-cinq communautés linguistiques de la France,* edited by G. Vermès. Vol. 1: *Langues régionales et langues non-territorialisées,* 381–413. Paris: L'Harmattan.

―――. 1989. Le développement du pentecôtisme chez les Tsiganes en France: Mouvement messianique, stéréotypes et affirmation d'identité. In *Actes du colloque international de l'AFA. Vers des sociétés pluriculturelles: Études comparatives et situation en France.* Paris: Éditions de l'Orstom.

―――. 1991a. *Django.* Montpellier, France: Éditions du Limon (Mood Indigo).

―――. 1991b. "Noi non ne parliamo . . .": Le relazioni tra i vivi e i morti in una comunita mānuš della Francia. In "Europa Zingara," edited by L. Piasere. Special issue, *La Ricerca folklorica,* 75–87.

―――. 1991c. Le miracle et la nécessité: À propos du développement du pentecôtisme chez les Tsiganes. *Archives de sciences sociales des religions* 73: 81–98.

―――. 1993. Questions pour l'étude du mouvement religieux pentecôtiste chez les Tsiganes. In *Ethnologie des faits religieux en Europe,* edited by N. Belmont and F. Lautman. Paris: Éditions du Comité des travaux historiques et scientifiques.

Yoors, Jan. 1990. *Tsiganes: Sur la route avec les Rom Lovara.* Paris: Phébus.

INDEX